An Integrative Model of Psychotherapy

A Case Study

Loredana Drobot
(Translated by Monica Rosu)

Published by Dolman Scott Ltd

Copyright © Loredana Drobot 2011
Translated by Monica Rosu

ISBN: 978-1-905553-84-6

Printed by Dolman Scott

www.dolmanscott.com

About the Author

Loredana Drobot graduated in Psychology at the University of West Timisoara – the Faculty of Sociology and Psychology – and did her doctoral studies in Educational Sciences at the University of Bucharest. She is currently PhD Associate Professor at the University "Eftimie Murgu" in Resita, specialising in psychopathology, psychotherapies, social assistance counselling and social pedagogy. She was trained in Transactional Analysis, clinical hypnosis, ericksonian psychotherapy and integrative psychotherapy. She is also the Scientific Secretary at the "Integrative Research, Counselling and Psychotherapy Association", psychotherapist, trainer and supervisor of the European Institute of Integrative Psychotherapy (Athens) and supervisor in educational psychology (The College of Romanian Psychologists). Her practical activity takes place in her own psychology practice.

Acknowledgements

Apart from the efforts of me, the success of any project depends largely on the encouragement and help of many others. I take this opportunity to express my gratitude to the people who have been instrumental in the successful completion of this project.

I would like to show my greatest appreciation to Alan Miller, Head of Psychology at St Luke's Healthcare Group. I can't say thank you enough for his tremendous help. Special mention is made of Nistor Becia, Amanda Becia and Liam Williams for their help in correcting the notes and invaluable assistance with publishing.

The author would also like to convey thanks to Monica Rosu for providing the English translation of this text.

I also want to thank to my family, especially my daughter Ioana, and friends for their understandings and support to me in completing this project. Without help of the particular type mentioned above I would face many difficulties while doing this.

Finally, the real joy for me now is that I can share some of that hard won wisdom with new therapists. Thank you, my readers, for allowing me to become, in a small way, part of the emotional healing you are doing with those who seek your help.

Loredana

Table of Contents

Foreword

To be asked to write the foreword of a book is a privilege for anyone, but to write a foreword to a book on psychotherapy is a special privilege; however, to be invited to write a foreword for a fellow mind and therapist from a different land, language, culture and tradition makes the experience unique. As a respected Romanian academic and therapist, Loredana Drobot has produced a work in English for the consumption of an international world; but a surprisingly small world when the reader examines the cases she presents to support her theories.

Initially reading this work, I was reminded of my background as a group worker in a psychotherapeutically orientated therapeutic community for young people back in the 1980s.
In those days, and in some ways, I was somewhat naive of how differing approaches in psychotherapy may overlap seamlessly or have similar content when using different descriptions. I believed my teachers and mentors to be firmly of the following of the 'Middle Group' of analysis, namely Bowlby and Winnicot (not forgetting Fairbairn and Balint); although I was able to reflect many years later that I had an unconscious awareness of Klein and her object relations theory. Silently there within this theoretical melee were Berne, Redl and Erikson. Within this work I see the same process for the author: different scholars and therapists, each with their own approach, but who contribute to a whole, holistic integration of therapy weaving in and out of the therapeutic experience.

On one occasion a number of us were dragged off to have an audience with the now discredited Bruno Bettleheim, who gave an interesting but perplexing lecture on classical interior design and how you should furnish your therapeutic establishment with priceless antiques. The relevance of this is that sometimes we forget how diverse our influences can be, but that all experience, regardless of what that experience may be, is a useful learning experience for therapists when that experience is the subject of reflection. This work is one of reflection that will help other therapists to learn from reflection.

Some years later, as a psychologist I worked in a prison therapeutic community where I had been immersed in the psychodynamic ways of Yallom in how to facilitate and interpret the workings of therapeutic groups, and yet I was also delivering cognitive behavioural approaches such as the Sex Offenders Treatment Programme.

When reading this work I was able to reflect that other therapists also use many different sources of theory to guide individual practice: Integrative psychotherapy, Psycho-synthesis, Eriksonian psychotherapy, short-term psychotherapy and the model of integrative counselling are all used to constuct this model of integrative psychotherapy.

I was also interested to see that Romania was not very different from the United Kingdom in that the general populace were equally confused as to the roles of psychiatrist and psychologist/psychotherapist, but more fundamentally that the most important factor of all is the relationship between the therapist and the client; everything else should follow this.

Loredana Drabot provides some unique client experiences and insights as she offers reflection, process and interpretation; but her contribution is unique in that she offers us all a psychotherapeutic perspective from Romanian eyes. Most of the time the cases, sentiments and experience are similar the world over, but there is an essence of her work that will remain forever Romanian.

Loredana's work undoubtedly will help break down any assumptions that therapeutic approaches in the old Eastern Bloc are substantially different from those seen in the West and will help to foster more collaboration across countries as we share our approaches to improving the human experience for those in distress.

Alan Miller, Head of Psychology
St. Luke's Healthcare Group
St. Luke's Hospital, Ebbw Vale. May 2011

Chapter I

Theoretic and methodological sources

1.1. Social environment and psychotherapy

The proposed model is a reflection of the way I work in my psychotherapy practice. I have often asked myself if the way I work with my clients, although each of them is unique, may be forwarded as a strategy of intervention. And thus I have tried to conceptualise each and every case as well as possible by transcribing most therapy sessions. Whenever I was writing about a case, I would discover something to solve for myself as a person, but in time I have also cultivated the power of observation concomitantly focused both on the client and on myself as therapist. Under that "external critical eye" I co-build the theoretic relationship between the client and myself. The critical eye retains all the aspects that I, as therapist, consider as worth being subjected to my reflection, supervision and group intervention with other therapist colleagues. As I, in my capacity of therapist, am responsible for the process from the therapy with the client, I also consider that the client may be determined to be responsible in the therapy, during the co-creation of the therapeutic relationship. I believe that the accountability of the client for therapy starts with the interest which I, as therapist, manifest for him or her, for what the client likes, for his or her world, etc. The interests for the activities the client likes also represents a gate through which I, the therapist, enter his or her reality, manifest interest for the products of his or her activity (drawings, poetry, photographs, etc), products that are subjected to the quality analysis. Therapists are not yet acquainted with the quality analysis in psychotherapy; unfortunately, research continues to focus mostly on quantity. I expect that every client may be a case for the qualitative research. The model I am about to present is perfectible and certainly an eclectic model from the viewpoint of the suggested techniques, which may belong to several orientations. What I attempt here is to

1

bring up for debate the importance of the therapist's functional flexibility, his or her ability to offer himself or herself as instrument and to select the techniques he or she considers the most appropriate here-and-now in his or her relationship with the client.

I shall thus present a frame sketch of intervention in counselling and psychotherapy, a difficult intervention as the client's uniqueness and issues cannot be forced into a pattern; nevertheless, my training in hypnosis, transactional analysis and integrative psychotherapy and especially the meeting with Ken Evans, whose image will always be in my soul and mind, made me dare sketch the model.

In some countries, seeing a psychologist has not been a habit; for instance, in Romania, for a long time the word "psychology" was excluded from the vocabulary. These past twenty years have constituted a period of effervescence in the world of psychotherapies: professional associations for the great therapy schools have been established, and one has founded the Romanian Federation of Psychotherapy, the College of Psychologists of Romania, etc. The joy and the feeling of belonging to an association have exalted therapists who, in their great majority, considered that the therapy in which they were training "represents … The Way, the Truth and the Life". Nevertheless, as each therapy occurred as a necessity to eliminate or reduce the negative aspects or to fill the voids of a form of dominant therapy, integrative psychotherapy in Romania appeared grace to the Romanian Association of Integrative Physiotherapy and the Romanian Institute of Integrative Psychotherapy. Later on, other associations were established with the term "integrative" in their denomination. The courage of Romanian founders, the commitment and effort of trainers in integrative psychotherapy to come to Romania from Europe and America, as well as certain psychotherapists' desire to learn and develop on the personal level, constituted the main driving forces in implementing and developing integrative psychotherapy in Romania.

However, people were not acquainted with the profession of psychologist, even though there was a certain image for the profession;

for a long time the psychologist had been mixed up with the psychiatrist, being shameful to admit that you go to or come from a counselling session with a psychologist. However, in the big cities the media and the increasingly numerous graduates in psychology make the psychologist's activity present in private practices, in organisations. The pressures are higher and higher, stress is increasing, the individual starts to seek specialised help. The therapist strives to find a place on the market and especially to work well, efficiently, on a short term basis. Among the most acute pressures acting upon psychotherapy and the therapist-client relation, we may list:

- time is money for both the client and the therapist;

- therapy can no longer by a luxury, it must be accessible to the individual who needs help;

- a psychologist is not a psychiatrist. Once I got the following answer from a 9-year-old client: "I told my schoolmates [my client used to tell everyone she was seeing a psychologist] that at the psychologist no medicine is given, no operations are performed, no injections are given";

- the pace of events is rapid: the client should quickly reintegrate into the social and professional environment. The list of pressures is long and will remain forever open.

I mentioned thus some of the social pressures felt by the client and the therapist and I arrived at the practice, the counselling and therapy room. In general, this is the map of the therapist's work reality; due to the aforementioned pressure, I was interested in conceiving a model of intervention in counselling and psychotherapy meant to represent for the client: the chance of receiving a quick help; the possibility of his or her empowerment before the problems he or she faces; the possibility of therapeutic change and learning; the validation in every-day life of knowledge and abilities acquired in therapy.

1.2. Theoretic and methodological sources of the forwarded model

The proposed model is a relational one in which the therapist-client relationship is fundamental. The theoretic sources of the model are the following:

1. Integrative psychotherapy, *the model proposed by Ken Evans, Maria Gilbert* (2000, 2005) from which I took the co-creation of the therapeutic relation and the importance of the client's contact break with himself or herself and with the world. The two authors, Ken Evans and Maria Gilbert, conceived a relational model of psychotherapy with the theoretic sources in the behavioural relational psychotherapy, gestalt theory, relational psychotherapy, existential phenomenology.

2. Psycho-synthesis, *elaborated by Assagioli* (1974, 1976), which I considered to be an integrative approach realised within the client's personality. The therapist sustains this internal process taking place in the client's personality, being attentive to the way he guides the sessions for developing the Self's energy. The therapist supports the client in his or her effort to make direct contact with personal feelings and emotions, and from this perspective the client may be both "immersed" into his inner self and "observer" of his own feelings.

3. Ericksonian psychotherapy – from which I took the use of dominant patterns in the therapist-client communication, as well as the dimensions of inducing the trance state: establishing the empathic resonance relation and developing the dominant (linguistic) hemisphere; the linguistic processing produced beyond the conscious level and the accessing of the non-dominant hemisphere (Bandler, R. & Grinder, J., 1975, 2007).

4. Short-term psychotherapy founded by De Shazer (1985), from which I took the rational elements of the therapeutic relationship; the therapist develops expectations and changes in the client, builds a new vision for a better future for the client (the client-therapist co-operation can be naturally and efficiently promoted) and develops a co-operative relationship with the client as part of finding the solutions to the problems. The focus is on what clients do, on what is good for them and less on what they think and what they stress as wrong.

5. The model of integrative counselling forwarded by S. Culley and T. Bond (2007), which offers an excellent guide on intervention and manifestation of the specialist's competencies and aptitudes in the relationship with the client.

I consider that the grounding of the intervention model on the above sources provides the therapist with flexibility in selecting the techniques of therapeutic intervention and with a better understanding of the empathic resonance relation. The selection and application of techniques cannot be done randomly, without being aware of the theories underlying them. I do promote a technical eclecticism from the domain of psychotherapies based on the therapist-client relation, of the techniques "accessing" the client's resources, and I bring it "here and now". The use of techniques from several psychotherapy models enables the therapist to work with a variety of clients and to observe the clients' uniqueness.

1.3. Therapist and therapeutic relationship

The therapeutic relationship is presented from the perspective of the theoretic and methodological sources of the forwarded model.

a) The integrative psychotherapy (K. Evans, M. Gilbert)
The therapist and the client are *co-creators of the therapeutic relationship* (K. Evans, M. Gilbert, 2005). The therapeutic relationship has the features of the humanist psychology, phenomenological, existentialist, and the therapist manifests:

- flexibility – in selecting the techniques from various psychotherapeutic orientations;

- presence – the therapist's capacities to be open to the client and at the same time present from the emotional and physical viewpoint;

- inclusion – the therapist's capacity to walk in the client's shoes, confirming his own experience and potential;

- inter-subjectivity – the therapist's capacity to understand the client's subjectivity and the significance of different interactions between his own personality and the client's. Other therapist's "acts" from the perspective of the model offered by K. Evans and M. Gilbert, based on a co-creative therapeutic relationship, are:

- contracting the therapy (location, confidentiality, number of sessions, cost, etc);

- observation and intervention at the initial stage of therapy, in the case of transfer and counter-transfer from the "It-It" relation (the client as observer for self and therapist). The therapist will be attentive to the client's needs of development, of being seen, helped and understood.

- the intervention in the case of a client's self-exposure with the generation of shame. Ken Evans claims that change occurs outside the support zone, change starts from the zone of the uncomfortable;

- diagnosing the client's experiences based on observations and analysis of the client's exposures as well as the hypotheses formulated by the therapist. Gary Yontef (1988) classifies the subject's experiences according to the time period: "here and now"; "there and now", "here and then" and "there and then". On their basis, Ken Evans (2000, p. 91) formulated the diagnostic model from the functional perspective, with focus on the functional and dysfunctional behaviour ("here and now" and "there and now"); relational perspective, with focus on contact, resistance and transfer

("here and there"); and developmental perspective, with focus on repetition and Self-object dimensions ("there and then");
- identification of the dysfunctional patterns blocking the client's contact with himself and the therapist. The therapist and the client reflect upon the dysfunctional behaviour, explore the behaviour and the defence mechanisms preserving the dysfunctional behaviour (desensitisation, introjection, retroflection, deflection and projection);

- the support for the client in experimenting with the feelings of sadness. Sometimes, touching the client, taking him by the hand, has a positive effect because it allows the client to reduce depression. There are opinions stating that the touching technique at such moments reflects a failure of empathy from the therapist's part, when unable to tolerate the client's sadness. Empathy and client's support by the therapist shape the client's capacity to tolerate sadness, which he will later on internalise (K. Evans, M. Gilbert, 2006);

- the expression of the therapist's feelings of counter-transfer in supervision and then in the process of therapy enables the establishment of objective transactions with the client, but their revealing should be done in moments of security during therapy. The consequence of expressing the counter-transfer feeling leads to the mutuality of the "I-You" therapeutic relationship, characterised by honesty, vulnerability and courage from the part of both sides (K. Evans, M. Gilbert, 2006). The "I-You" relationship allows the client to overcome his or her initial patterns and to open towards the therapist.

All the above aspects are detailed in the works of authors K. Evans and M. Gilbert. I present them briefly and only what I consider that I use in the practice of the model I put forward. I point out that when I work with a client I do not necessarily use all the diagnosis formulations from the functional, relational and developmental perspective.

b) The psycho-synthesis elaborated by Assagioli
From Assagioli's psycho-synthesis I considered it necessary to take the following aspects:

- when one identifies a dysfunctional pattern blocking the client from himself and the world, the therapist can identify those sub-personalities (structure constellations or agglomeration of attitudes, wills, habit patterns, similar to the "complexes" from psychoanalysis or games from the transactional analysis) responsible for the engagement of mechanisms (deflection, retroflection, etc). Sub-personalities help an immature organism to face reality, to survive; but in the long run they become inefficient means of satisfying needs: the person grows up and develops other resources. The energy used by such a sub-personality is limited and cannot be used in other forms of manifestation. By psycho-synthesis one attempts to release those energies of sub-personality in order to use the entire personality;

- the most important cognition of psycho-synthesis in therapy is to realise the disinvestment of identification. Clients let themselves be dominated by what is identified, identify themselves with partial aspects of their own person as though they were living by compartments. For instance, the client identifies himself with the sub-personality having triggered the blockage or interruption of the contact with himself or with the world. The therapist teaches the client how to walk away from sub-personalities, how to "move" them. The clients may also identify themselves with social roles. The concept of role itself is similar to that of sub-personality. I consider that there is a correspondent in the Transactional Analysis of the disinvestment of sub-personalities through the analysis of the functional states of the 2nd degree self and through behavioural, social, historical and phenomenological diagnosis of the self states.

The client's identification may be reached also with certain feelings. Thus, first of all, the client, with the therapist's help, grace to the qualities of the aforementioned therapeutic relations, will realise he is

8

in a blockage; then he is helped to understand his experiences as a result of certain identifications with sub-personalities, roles, sentiments; and eventually he will proceed to their disidentification;

- the therapist is the "mirror" of the client's will, helps him discover the attitudes controlling him, the resources for expressing the Self's will. The clients who identify themselves with sub-personalities cannot make decisions without coming into conflict with other parts of personality.

By will the client opens himself before the therapist, before the others and thus the "I-You" relationship is shaped. If the client's motivation is not developed enough, then the therapist must seek a modality enabling the client to return to the task fulfilment.

Sub-personalities have a narrow vision on life; reality is perceived only through the prism of the sub-personality with which the client identifies himself, without taking into consideration the other parts. The motivated sub-personality attempts to escape the others if it feels threatened, but the Self's will acts in an integrative manner, the Self neither ignores nor denies the other parts of personality, but takes into account the needs of the whole.

The therapist's role is to work together with the client and to "transfer" energy from one sub-personality with which the client identifies himself on the self level (for instance, the performing sub-personality of the client asks for the therapist's help to eliminate the idle personality, or a dependent client may passively expect that the therapist solves the problem or guides him, instead of being open or participating in the guiding process);

- The therapist, grace to the relationship he builds with the client, the relation the two co-create, helps with the emotional release. If the feelings are blocked, their energy should be creatively released.
Some people need therapy to release powerful emotions that are not totally expressed, as they consume considerable energy. Such emotions are related to the failed relationships with parental figures

or to traumatic situations from the person's life. The true healing occurs through forgiveness and reconciliation. Forgiveness comes after the compassion feeling occurred as a consequence of the "discussion" between the client and the "sub-personality" which identified itself with the introjected parent, aggressor, etc. The stage of abreaction or violent release of powerful emotions is not necessary for all clients. The clients with less dramatic traumatic experiences and with feelings associated to the "parental imago" experience emotional release gradually and less dramatically. In the case presented in the second part of the work, I shall show how I intervened for the disinvestment of a sub-personality and how energy is transferred to the entire self.

c) The Ericksonian psychotherapy
Milton Erickson was a master in inducing hypnotic trances. References to the manner in which he worked remain to posterity in the grace of the writings of his collaborators and disciples. I do not intend insisting on the way hypnosis is realised by M. Erickson; nevertheless I consider it necessary to mention some features of the therapeutic relationship. A psychotherapist who considers himself integrative should not ignore the features of the hypnotic languages: voice, intonation, pauses, conjunctions, prepositions, metaphors, jokes, the two-level communication, interpersonal technique, etc. Hypnosis in general is a technique supposing much endeavour in its assimilation. All psychotherapies are based on hypnotic elements. I shall present the sequence of the aspects I considered important in facilitating the therapist-client relationship, from the perspective of the Ericksonian therapy for: the re-establishment of the client's contact with himself and the others, the disinvestment of identifications, the emotional release, the Self strengthening, etc.

Establishing the empathic resonance relation between the therapist and the client (Bandler, R. & Grinder, J., 2007) constituted the central theme I took into the present model and:

1- it starts with the therapist's welcoming of the client's model on the world; we do not force the client to accept anything new, we do not make him deny his beliefs, convictions, because we facilitate his resistances. The therapist meets the client on his territory, welcomes his model on the world, accepts it and exploits it to the maximum;

2- it supposes accepting and using any manifestation of the client, the latter's role is maximised and the therapist role is minimised;

3- it accesses the dominant hemisphere in order to induce the hypnotic trance: "the deep hypnosis is the level allowing the subject to act in an optimum way and directly on the plane of the unconscious, without the interference of the conscious mind" (Milton Erickson);

4- it identifies the client's dominant system of representation: visual (he uses predicates with reference to visual representations), kinaesthetic (he uses predicates from the domain of kinaesthetic representations), auditory (he uses predicates from the domain of acoustic representations).

The most efficient therapists are those who use the client's system of representations. Each person creates models of the world, which considerably differ from reality as such and one individually operates with representations of the world essentially different from the others. The formal models or metamodels are built so that they might present configuration patterns used for drawing reality maps;

5- it uses the verbal empathy. Two efficient descriptive general categories are involved here:

a) description of the momentary experience seizable at the client – the therapist realises clear visual and acoustic dissociations while he observes and listens to the client, in order to incorporate them into the process of representation of his behaviour ("you breath in … breath out …, etc"). The therapist uses his position, movements of the body, intonation, rhythm in accordance with the client, uses words and syntagms similar to the client's. All these are essential elements for the rapid and efficient inducing of trance. The response channels, reactions, experience of the client, all are in accordance with the client's reactions. The therapist aims at communicating with the client in an optimum way, issues assertions that can be verified by the client and puts them in relation with an affirmation describing the behaviour the client demands. The guaranteed elements connecting the ongoing experience of the client and what the client will experience in the near future during trance are: the simple conjunction, the implicit causal clause and the cause-effect relations.

b) description of the client's unobservable experiences – the therapist uses the modelling linguistic principles in order to put the client before a series of vague, ambiguous assertions: "… you may become aware of a certain significance …". The therapist's referrals focus on one of the experiences unobservable for the client.

Milton Erickson used further techniques allowing the establishment of the relation of empathic resonance:

- violation of selective restrictions – a technique resembling that of the absence of the referential index, the client has the task to assign other significance to expressions to replace the initial illogism;

- suppression – situation in which the sequence from the deep structure has no correspondent at the surface, "… and you continue to be confused … and indeed", where the "confused" predicate shows that someone asks questions on something specific, but at the surface structure no mention is made about who wonders, what he wonders at; these sequences of the sense have been suppressed. The listener (client) should contribute with the missing information;

- nomination – linguistic phenomenon related to the absence of the referential and suppressing index consists in the representation of a word expressing an action (a predicate) with words encoding an effect (a noun), "… a certain sensation …". The noun "sensation", although derived from the verb "to sense", associates a vast quantity of information. The information regarding who senses, what or how the subject of sensing feels, was lost. Thus, one has renounced to referential indices on the sensor, on persons or on the sensed thing, and the person (client) considers that the expression applies to the experience he is living at that particular moment.

Among the verbs (predicates) useful for establishing the relation of empathic resonance (non-specific verbs), M. Erickson mentioned: to wonder, to think, to perceive, to feel, to know, to experiment, to understand, to become aware of, to remember, etc.

- "mind reading" enables therapists to pretend they are aware of the client's thoughts and feelings without specifying the process triggering the respective awareness: "… I know you ask yourself …".

Trance inducing supposes for M. Erickson also the client's suggestioning, not necessarily by direct training, but also by means of using certain modelling principles of the natural languages. In this respect one uses the principle of presupposition: "… yes, and I wonder if you have remarked the chair on which you will soon sit as comfortably as possible …".

Presuppositions are the linguistic equivalent of what is currently called presumptions, both being basic organisational principles without which the information presented makes no sense: "… I wonder if you are aware of the fact that you are experiencing a profound state of trance …".

M. Erickson uses "to become aware" in order to give meaning to the syntagm "a deep state of trance" and to accept it as truth grace to the adverb "profoundly". One may combine the presuppositions "… Are you profoundly living a state of trance?" (by "profoundly" the experiencing is stressed, not the trance *in se*), and the client does not question the truth of the assertion "you are in a state of trance".

The modelling principles of the natural language are necessary for reaching an indirect communication with the client. The indirect communication with the client enables:

- the avoidance of resistances;

- the client's liberty of (unconsciously) choosing fragments of communication as lines;

- the establishing of the unconscious level of communication, but also the conscious one, in order to avoid intrusion. The client may participate much more dynamically in the inducing and experiencing of the trance.

Among the techniques used in reaching an indirect communication with the client, one also lists:

- conversational postulates: the therapist does not order the client what to do, he prefers to ask him, "Can you put your hand on your hips?";

- the patterns of the included inferior structures: the therapist indirectly asks the client a question and does not expect an answer, but the client usually replies, senses the communication as a question: "… I wonder if you really feel at ease …".
The included inferior structures are very powerful modalities to orient the client's experience and are combined with the technique of analogical mark.
The analogic mark supposes the use of the non-linguistic modality of communication in order to distribute and identify the linguistic communication into distinct message units (change of intonation, speech pauses, etc): "… I used to know a man who really knew how to feel good …".

Sometimes, rather seldom, the clients are aware of such analogous permutations, and then the result of communication is the double communication (the story the therapist tells for the conscious side of the mind and the order to feel good transmitted to the unconscious side).

M. Erickson uses visual and acoustic lines in order to mark communication in an analogical manner.

I mention here part of the techniques used by M. Erickson perceived by the therapist as useful in the therapeutic session, because, when the specialist decides to use hypnosis, mastering the two-level language and communication is extremely important.

d) The short-term psychotherapy founded by De Shazer (1985)

De Shazer mentioned that "*therapists must know what to avoid doing and that what the clients did is usually the most vivid illustration of what should not be done. Anyway, as the clients have often to overcome the difficulty to formulate the purpose, the therapists must build the problems so that he reaches the purpose or vision on the future*" (De Shazer, S., 1985, p. 56). The client's discontentments may seem trivial to the therapists and there may also be things the client does not complain about, but may be considered important or are communicated to the therapist as discontentments: "*discontent becomes a problem as long as the client and the therapist can do something about it*".

Clients want to change, but some think that the ideas about how to change do not match and it is difficult to label it as "resistance" when the client in fact wishes to change. There are situations when the therapist himself recommends the client to another therapist, because he perceives him as "opaque / resistant". De Shazer suggests: "*first I correlated the present to the future (ignoring the past), then I congratulated the clients on what they were doing, this was efficient for them, and then – once they knew we were on their side we could make a suggestion for something new, that we considered good for them*" (op. cit., p. 15). The clients respond when they receive such a message. Consequently, the therapist is co-creator of the therapeutic relation and is focused upon:

- the client's desire of change;
- the transformation of the client's discontentments into problems.

The system of the client's discontentments includes (op. cit., p. 27):

- a sequence of behaviour;
- significances assigned by the client to certain situations;
- the frequency with which a discontentment occurs;
- the location where the discontentment occurs;
- the extent to which the discontentment is involuntary;
- the persons directly involved in the discontentment;
- the question "Who is to blame?" or "What triggers the discontentment?";
- the social factors involved, such as: work, dwelling, family, economic status;
- the client's degree of emotional and psychological involvement;
- the client's past;
- the client's predictions related to the future;
- the client's expectations.

We remark that any change of an element triggers possible modification in other elements: a change redimensions another change. The client may have certain favourite factors in describing the problem and the therapist is very careful to note the mentioned factors. Each factor may be considered as "doors" leading to solutions, each discontentment is different, and the solutions are those with the best locks and keys. Several doors may lead to the same solutions or to different solutions, or any door may lead to a dark alley. The therapist and the client must realise which door can still be opened.

Creating the hope in the client that the change will be beneficial and then several alternatives of the future may occur. The therapeutic change is an interactional process between the therapist and the client. It is not something the therapist does to the client as though the client were a "recipient" and therapy is not surgery or TV mending.

Clients "*do not bring their problems in a labelled box, as a type x problem, so that when they present it to the therapist they are already in the process of redefining those problems"* (Emerson & Messinger, 1977). The therapist thinks of the interactional activity of therapy as a co-operating process, in which the client and the therapist build together the solution to the problem: *"patients can only share a rather confused amount of what they think and you listen with your own knowledge and you don't know what they are saying, but it is better to become aware you do not know. Then you must do something to induce a change in the patient ... any small change, because the patient wants it. We shall not stop to measure the implications of the change. The patient will accept it as change and then he will follow it, and the change will transform him according to his own needs. ... It is like rolling a snowball down a mountain; at first it is only a small snowball, but as it rolls it becomes larger and larger ... and turns into an avalanche on the mountain format* (Gordon & Meyers-Anderson, 1981, pp. 16-17).

The therapist thus thinks of the interaction with the client as a co-operation activity, in which both of them build the solution of the problem. The change I propose to the clients occurs when I suggest to them that they write about what they feel, how they think the therapeutic relation is going, to bring a product of their activity to the next session (poetry, drawings, diary fragments, etc).

e) The model of integrative counselling proposed by S. Culley and T. Bond (2007)

S. Culley and T. Bond (2007) conceived an excellent intervention "guide", useful for the therapist in counselling and therapy. Establishing a functional therapeutic relationship is a goal considered fundamental in the therapeutic intervention and can be reached only if the therapist has the required competencies and aptitudes, if he has reached an appropriate level of personal training, development and supervision in integrative psychotherapy (within the proposed model). The client invests trust and energy in the therapeutic relationship and on this basis he starts to solve his problems.

I included the model conceived by S. Culley and T. Bond into the sources of the integrative model as it provides a structuring of intervention strategies and the therapist's aptitudes necessary for establishing a functional therapist-client relationship.

1) The therapist's intervention strategies necessary in the integrative model above and taken from the model forwarded by S. Culley and T. Bond (2007) are the following:

- exploration, in order to help the client in the analysis of his preoccupations and concerns;

- focusing on the client's issues in order to hierarchise the problem, to set a certain order in the occurrence of the problem and to identify the moment the problems appeared;

- concrete and specific communication necessary for an active listening in order to grasp the generalisations, distortions, omissions, ambiguities from the client's communications;

- challenging the client to formulate a new perspective on problems;

- establishment of the evaluation goals or objectives in order to assess the changes triggered by therapy and to evaluate, on the imagination level, the expected results aimed at in the future;

- planning of future actions together with the client;

- support for the change of behaviour and assuring the client that he copes well with daily challenges;

- finalisation of therapy allotting the time necessary to the client to overcome the feeling of sadness and loss of the therapeutic relationships, as the clients frequently become anxious before the idea the therapy is about to end.

2) The therapist's competencies and skills necessary in the creation and preservation of a functional relationship with the client, taken from the model elaborated by S. Culley and T. Bond, included into the integrative model, are as follows:

- *Listening and attention skills.* The therapist shows the client he is listening to him by:

- listening and keeping silent – silence can also be a modality of speaking and a way of creating a balance between the client's support through words and offering the client the necessary space for reflection;
- breaking the silence is done by formulating questions such as: *"How are you feeling now?"*, *"What are you thinking about?"*, *"What is happening with you now?"*;
- exploiting the personal reactions, feelings and thoughts so that the clients can see that the therapist himself is no stranger to the client's emotions;
- eliminating the obstacles in the way of an active listening.

The therapist shows the client he is paying attention by:

- the posture adopted, comfortable, open;
- the visual contact, maintained during the entire therapy, but not by staring at the client;
- face expression;
- spatial position.

- *Reflexive skills.* The therapist, through his reflective skills, builds an environment propice to communication, develops the client's confidence in the therapeutic relation, follows the thoughts and feelings of the client, can verify if he has understood the client or not, etc. The following are included in the category of reflexive skills:
- repetition, by stressing some emotionally loaded words or short sentence. The repetition of a word allows directing the answer.

The therapist must be cautious and should not use repetition abusively, as the client may get lost in his assertions;

- paraphrase supposes the message rephrasing, the client has the possibility to "hear again" what he is told and understands or rephrases his assertions. Paraphrasing validates the therapeutic relationship (Drobot, L., *Integrative counselling and psychotherapy*, 2008, p. 124).

Among the goals of paraphrasing, we may list: verification of the therapist's perception of the client's words, the validation of the empathic understanding of the client, getting information on how the client perceives himself without imposing any discussion to the client.

S. Culley and T. Bond (2007) offer some landmarks for the therapist when he wishes to use paraphrasing:

- to provide a clear perception of the client's assertions;

- to avoid defining the client's words;

- to avoid being judgemental, sarcastic, to be respectful with the client;

- to avoid imitating the client by using identical words, i.e. to use his own words in paraphrasing;

- to avoid adding things;

- to be short and direct in paraphrasing;

- to keep a constant tone of voice.

- summarising or abstracts realised by the therapist are longer paraphrases. The useful abstracts or summaries are short, concrete, offering a clear vision on the therapeutic intervention up to that moment. Summarising aims at: clarifying the client's sentiments: *"I'd like to check with you if I have understood well ..."*, and then offering a summary of the assertions, providing opportunities to correct misunderstandings, to add or rethink the client's accounts, finalising the therapy session to confirm what the client agreed to before the following session, forwarding some discussion topics for the future sessions: *"I was thinking about the last session discussion ... you were talking about ... I wonder if you wish to continue or to approach other issues ..."*.

- Argumentative skills. The therapist uses such skills too in order to be more direct when he paraphrases and summarises.

The manner in which the therapist addresses the client when he argues is passive or integrative, under the form of questions:

- Open questions, in order to encourage the client's involvement under the form of "Yes" or "No" answers. It is recommended to avoid too open questions;
- Hypothetical questions, inviting the client to formulate hypotheses, imagine the future and formulate the consequences of the therapy: "What do you think might happen if you were to say no?", "How would you react if I controlled your anxiety?". The therapist demands the construction of images and by the exploration of those images insights occur about the issues avoided by the client: "If you imagine yourself as knowing how you might behave, what would you say?";
- "Why?" questions are not recommended to be used too often. The "Why?" question blocks the client, does not help him find new possibilities of action. Some clients do not want to understand the "reasons why", are reluctant to search for answers, are interested only in their dysfunctional behaviour;
- closed questions do not require an exploration on the part of the client. The frequent use of closed questions places the

- "either ... or" questions are restrictive and offer the client only two options: "Will you tell him tomorrow or will you wait until you are asked?", and the answer may be "Neither, I don't think I will tell him anything";
- multiple questions are not recommended, as they determine the client's confusion. The client may require clarifications from the therapist or he will often not know which question to answer;
- questions determining the client's response, as they are formulated so that the desired answer can be guessed, as well as beliefs, values, sentiments, experiences. Some answers are transmitted by the therapist by non-verbal indices: "You should not think like that", or "You should not wish that".

The skills of the counsellor or therapist are essential for the here-and-now understanding, validation and acceptance of the client. In Transactional Analysis we, as therapists, act from the state of Adult Ego. A counsellor, in the relation with the client, expresses the feelings of his or her own Ego states necessary for creating an authentic therapeutic relationship, but the respective states are supervised by the Adult Ego state.

Chapter II

Therapeutic objectives and strategies

2.1 Evaluations in Counselling and Therapy

It may seem rather strange for me to present therapeutic objectives in a model of therapeutic intervention, knowing that each client is unique, his problems are unique. The objectives I propose are considered "guiding lights" over the tormented sea of the client's soul. The client's uniqueness requires flexibility in establishing the categories of objectives in the therapeutic process. These categories may be related to other objectives generated by the client's here-and-now situation, by the stage of the therapeutic relation, etc. During the first session one specifies not only the therapeutic framework, but one contracts also the general objective of therapy, counselling, objective "negotiated" with the client. The client has his goals for which he came to counselling or therapy, goals he negotiates with the therapist; but the latter in his turn has to reach certain objectives from the viewpoint of the therapeutic process. The present chapter addresses these objectives; we may consider them similar to methodological goals or objectives.

I tried to group the therapeutic goals or objectives into four large categories: establishing the therapeutic relationship; identifying the moment when the client's contact with himself and with the world has been "broken"; developing the "I-You" relationship (the therapist as interface between the client and the world); and starting the client into the professional and social world. It is known that, due to the individual differences among people, it is impossible to propose a single therapeutic model. Grounding the proposed model reflects, as mentioned before, part of my training as psychotherapist, my individual study and the activity in my own practice. I adapted the interventions to the clients' needs and the interventions were customised. I consider the therapist's intuition and flexibility to be of great importance. What I suggest does not mean that I am adept at strict intervention algorithms; I perceive the proposal offered as a synthesis of some empathetically validated landmarks, orienting me in making some correct decisions during interventions. It is not the client who adapts to the intervention, but the therapist respects and steps with decency and consideration into the therapeutic relation. Each client has a unique therapy and sometimes his healing "escapes" the therapist, who asks himself: "But ... how?", it was probably enough for the client that he was not alone ... And yet, "let us hurry a little, the client will heal by himself anyway" should not occur in the conception of professionals. Although the therapist has a representation of the intervention to apply, first of all he keeps in mind that the moment the client has come through the door, the most efficient intervention is based on his needs and the recourse to the therapeutic manoeuvres adequate to his needs. For instance, a client who comes to therapy on his own will and insistently demands counselling or comes at the recommendation of the doctor X with complaints formulated in a desperate manner that he is anxious, has panic attacks, at the end of the first session, if I have succeeded in building a therapeutic relation, I sometimes apply the metaphor of the "favourite spot" to initiate a possible contact of the client with his own body, in order to better recognise the signals sent by the client's body to himself and to start him learning a little from relaxation.

Evaluations from therapy

The therapist has, at the end of therapy, numerous landmarks of the client's motivation, i.e. the sign of coming a long way from: passiveness to activity, dependency relation to independence (or relative independence); subordination position to equal relations, state with few possibilities of action to states with more possibilities of action, novel superficial interest to mature interest, living in the past or in the moment of contact "break" to living in the present and future; obscure, diffuse manifestations of the Ego to controlled manifestations.

The aforementioned "signs" are built gradually and I recommend therapists to take them into account at the evaluations during therapy. The evaluations during therapy or the partial evaluations are important and mobilise the client for his personal awareness when they are highlighted and expressed by real behaviours; the client experiences a feeling of contentment, as he has the gradual proof of his change. Sometimes the client does not grasp these changed behaviours, and then the therapist "gently" underlines them, by direct and indirect suggestions: he suggests the client be more receptive and attentive to his conduct manifestations, to retain them, to weigh them and bring them to the following session. For some clients the therapist formulates items of "homework" such as writing down these behaviours and, although they do not always put them down, at the following session they register them in the memory and talk about them. Under an integrative form, the therapy sessions begin with the question, "I really wondered what you did, felt, experienced last week …". At the partial evaluations I focus on the following (Drobot, L., *Relational psychotherapy*, 2009):

- *the cognitive domain* – acquisitions, cognitive experiences, change contracting, "old" schemes practised, "new" schemes practised, etc;
- *the behavioural domain* – the old and new behaviours, the assertive behaviours, the courage manifested by creating a behaviour in the family, at the place of work;
- *the affective domain* – currently manifested feelings, introjections, if they were or were not admitted by the client, what he would have wished to express affectively and did not, the search, together with the client, for the significance of such behaviours, where the blockage occurred, if it was or was not admitted by the client, etc;
- *the physiologic domain* – muscular tensions, precise pains, shaking, insomnia, etc. One client described her physiologic manifestation at the first session with, "I feel a stomach 'bending' and this bending and doubt is going up to the heart … to the head". I asked the client to elaborate, if possible, on

25

the stomach "bending" and then she slightly inclined her torso forward. The gesture indicated, in fact, cramps, stomach pains; but also the bending as insecurity, as existential experience, doubt on the sentimental and cognitive level (heart, head). The client was not just bending, she was doubting not only herself but the entire world.

On the last therapy session the client has already indirectly learned about what plans he will speak in general; the last session is the moment of his "victory", the moment when the clients are fluent, coherent in expression, assume responsibilities, admit that life is a personal challenge, are cautious and "full of love for themselves". Even since the first session, when I orient his look towards himself, I mention that taking care of himself, respecting himself, loving himself is not a proof of selfishness. If he is at peace and content with himself, then he is better for himself, but also for those near him; can be a better friend, spouse, professional. For this very fact the time would be used in therapy for the Self, and after that he may become better for himself and for others. On the occasion of evaluations I also insist on the difference between the client's needs and the needs of others. The client who comes to therapy has difficulties in telling his needs from the needs of the others, is searching for himself and gets lost. He had lost the landmark towards himself; in its place there remained a "casing". I tell the client that walking through the world does not mean being alone; it supposes being with himself, but first we must search for this "himself" inside him and then we shall find the resources too, the reservoir of his strength. The therapeutic relationship is the fundament of the interventions in which one builds or rebuilds the client's contact with himself and with the world, but with respect; in the dance I start with the client for several months I do not forget to mention from the first session and during partial evaluations that the laurels of victory are theirs; the therapist is the instrument enabling them to rebuild themselves. I plant the seeds of expectations of change and healing on the very first session and I "already" retire to anonymity and quietly leave their rebuilt life. During the last session I congratulate them on their achievements and I recommend them to guard with respect all they have acquired and gained with such effort and pain. They did nothing wrong in life; many clients feel guilty and experience a feeling of guilt, then I mention that the client had only the possibility to learn. Moreover, on the occasion of partial evaluations I remind my clients that day by day the every-day life validates them and what they learned in the practice is validated the moment they get out of it. In some situations there is the tendency of the client to call me between sessions. I let them do it, but most often clients do not call me, and during the following session they mention this intention. I ask them what stopped them from calling me and they say they also thought of the possibility of solving the problem themselves and they told themselves: "what the heck, I can do it". I consider that such situations are excellent opportunities to congratulate them on having behaved admirably, on their being on the way opened towards the world, telling them that, anyway, they would not have found out how to do it even if they had called. The client assumed the responsibility of his own actions without seeking help outside.

2.2. Categories of therapeutic objectives

In the introduction I mentioned the four large categories of therapeutic objectives. The success of a therapeutic intervention depends on many factors, but from my experience I consider the following factors to be most important:

- the therapist's focus on the client's needs;

- formulation and flexibility in building habits, in accordance with the client's needs;

- the client's motivation for change and therapeutic learning;

- fulfilment of the client's expectations;

- identification, activation of the client's trust in his own resources;

- identification of the modalities of therapeutic interventions (methods, techniques) for activating resources;

- identification of the intervention modalities (methods, techniques) for reaching the set therapeutic goals or objectives.

The efficiency of therapy depends on the therapist's capacity to build a therapeutic strategy meant to customise the concrete intervention.

The categories of goals may include, as mentioned before, other objectives determined also by the client's needs, which can by reached by selecting appropriate techniques. Thus, the therapist's creativity and flexibility are his main advantages. From this perspective, the proposed model (the viewpoint of the variety of the techniques used) reflects the technical eclecticism. The proposed integrative model has identified and mentioned theoretic sources, but also a vast range of methods and techniques, with the possibility of including some more according to the therapist's flexibility and knowledge, i.e. a technical eclecticism.

The model is mixed, theoretic-eclectic, at the interlacing of other models and orientations and is not a trans-theoretic model.

I already mentioned that it is impossible to elaborate a small model, a rigid map of intervention to succeed in solving the client's problems. Consequently, the basic principle of the mixed theoretic-eclectic model proposed is that the therapist practises a responsible flexibility in selecting techniques, in performing interventions adapted to the client's needs and not to his momentary inspiration of floating intuition.

The process or technique used is triggered by the "data" offered by the client in the practice.
In the attempt to establish ataxonomy of therapeutic objectives, I identified four categories of therapeutic goals or objectives.

2.2.1. Objective I (or the first category of objectives) – establishing the therapeutic relationship

When and where. The telephone conversation before the first session

The construction of a therapeutic relation sometimes begins even before the clients come to the practice, by phone, when they wish to schedule a session. The family members often call and ask for an appointment for the client. In such situations I demand to talk to the client in person. After I introduce myself, I ask the client to express, if possible, the problem for which he or she desires to come to therapy. The client's decision to make a first contact with the therapist confirms the fact that he took control as regards the solution to his problem. The therapist has the possibility to "read" the mind of those expectations, as he gets valuable indications about the client's inner world and about the opportunity to work in therapy. There are other clients who claim they do not expect very much from therapy; this is a further reason to come to therapy, which will be analysed together with the client during the first session. The therapist thus delimits the therapy expectations of those who call on behalf of the client and the expectations of the client himself.

The first contact with the client constitutes a conceptualisation session: the therapist, in his turn, proves if he is a good listener or not.

The first therapy session

This first session is loaded with significance for the co-creators of the therapeutic relation. The therapist, at the first session:

- observes the client as a person and not a patient;

- confirms the initial telephone contact (if there was one);

- contracts the future therapeutic sessions: the precise setting of the session duration, the presentation of the process (permission or refusal to record), application of questionnaires to gather further information (I use them very rarely), making sure if the client has some questions about the therapy;

- describes the modality to proceed, without using jargon;

- avoids labelling the client: "My purpose is to help you solve your problem, not to judge you". Thus, the therapist expresses loyalty towards the client, offers some indications about the possible changes that may occur during therapy. The therapist demonstrates the client's acceptance and builds anequilibrium between offering information about him and the client's acceptance;

- explores the client's current problems (those issues considered important by the client). As the client explores his problems, he discovers new aspects, more painful, more profound. By exploring the problems and locating them in the context of the client's life, a conceptualisation can be formulated.

The therapist is guided by questions such as:
"What problems does the client stress?";
"Which implications of the problems have not been mentioned by the client yet?";
"What persons are also involved?";
"When do the problems occur?";
"What mechanisms does the client activate before the problems?";
"What is the client's network of social support?";
"How has the client coped with the problems before coming to the practice?".

Consequently, the therapist collects information about the client's motivation for change; he studies, searches, identifies the factors having affected the client's behaviour, asks the client about the previous medical tests, asks the client if he has been in therapy before (if yes, the therapist may require permission to consult his file at the former therapist), he observes if the client had any negative therapeutic experiences in the past.

The therapist comprehends if the client's problem or trauma included the biologic or temperament factors and predispositions, other previous trauma, as the current problems may be unconsciously associated with the traumas of the past. The therapist should exhibit attention and a lot of caution when he investigates the history of the trauma, especially in the case of post-traumatic troubles and dissociate suffering.

For instance, the clients who suffered sexual abuse are very brief in expression, the revealing of the trauma account takes time and when it is done the client relives part of the emotional burden. As a therapist, I abstain myself from any comment or suggestion. I am there and show my presence there through the way I listen; I am attentive. In the end I thank the client for having found the force and trust to share his pain with me.

- asks questions to identify the client's inner resources;

I usually start with the request to describe the timetable of a normal day in the client's life, then I ask him to account a situation in the future when the problem is solved. Some clients cannot imagine such situations. Then I ask them to talk about a situation in the past, a happy situation when the problem was not yet present. Then I rephrase for the client the request to imagine a happy situation in the future. I found out that most of the time the client does not exhibit resistance or reluctance any more. I avoid interpretations, but I rephrase the example given by the client with the request to "correct me if I omit anything ...";

- synthesises the significance of therapy, its role in the client's life, especially as a possibility of self-exploration and self-awareness. The therapist recalls the therapeutic contract and the necessity to observe its terms, and if an unforeseen event occurs, the client is asked to notify the annulment of the therapy.

The conclusion of the first therapy session is thus a self-awareness opportunity for the client and the therapist's opportunity to start a new "dance on the stage of social life with another partner".

- assures the confidentiality of therapy. Confidentiality is essential to enable the client to talk freely and openly about his problems. The limits of confidentiality are set by negotiation with the client. In some situations it is recommended to say, "What you say or do here is confidential, but I am telling you, as I tell other clients, that if I find there is the risk of your harming yourself or others, I will do all that is required to talk first to you and then to other persons";

- reduces the client's resistance by offering certain answers, such as: "I realise you do not want to be here. Nevertheless, I am curious to know why you are reluctant to receive my help". In fact, the conversation is opened and there is a chance to get to know the client's desires;

- provides the client with information about the state of being absorbed, of focusing attention, of dissociating (the state of shock), states he knows from daily life. For instance, when he watches an interesting TV show, when he reads a book and is absorbed by what he reads, when he is on the verge of falling asleep (the border between vigil and sleep state). The therapist may also collect information about the client's favourite places (nature, seaside, mountain), important aspects for the therapy when he intends to provoke hypnotic indications. In this educational phase regarding the hypnotic techniques, the therapist in fact prepares the client for hypnosis: all the forms of hypnosis are actually self-hypnosis, hypnosis resembles the relation between a guide and a pioneer, hypnosis is an ability and can be learned by practice. The counter-indications of hypnosis are also mentioned, i.e. in the organic brain damages, paranoid depressions, schizophrenia, structures of fragile Egos, cognitive troubles, etc. The therapist going for the application of hypnotic techniques will practise a respectful, collaborative, permissive style; the therapist's experience and thinking are the most important in making the decision whether to subject the client to hypnosis or not.

2.2.2. Objective II (or the second category of objectives). Identifying the moment when the gestalt cycle was broken, the client's contact with himself and implicitly with the world

a) Breaking of the contact with himself

A number of two or three sessions are necessary to identify the moment of the break of contact with himself, the moment when the client blocked the contact with his inner self. P. Clarkson (1989) graphically plots the contact in the initial phase of the A-B gestalt cycle.

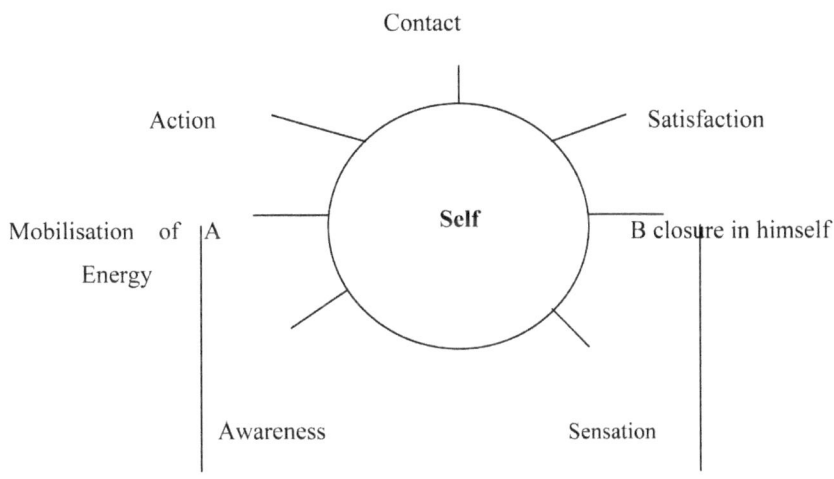

Contact

Action   Satisfaction

Mobilisation   of |A   **Self**   B closure in himself

Energy

Awareness   Sensation

Blockage of the client's contact with himself and the therapist in the A-B initial phase of the
gestalt cycle

Fig. no. 1 The pattern of a dysfunctional behaviour

Source. Clarkson P., (1989) Apud K. Evans, M. Gilbert (2006, p. 93)

The therapist will be concerned, together with the client, with the identification of the defence mechanism that maintains the pattern of the dysfunctional behaviour:

- desensitisation – by which the client "annuls" the sensations of the supported mechanism due to inappropriate emotional introjected messages ("It is not normal for a boy to cry");

- introjection – aimed at internalising the messages from parents, authorities, etc. Here the therapist practising T.A. may intervene with the analysis of the 1st and 2nd order Ego states;

- retroflection – by which emotions are retained within the body and consequently the client becomes rigid, with weak breath, clenched jaws, tight fists, etc;

- deflection – by which the client interrupts the contact with the therapist;
projection – by which the client projects the criticism towards the therapist and protects himself against contact ("I don't understand how a stranger can understand my problem", etc) (see Figure no. 2).

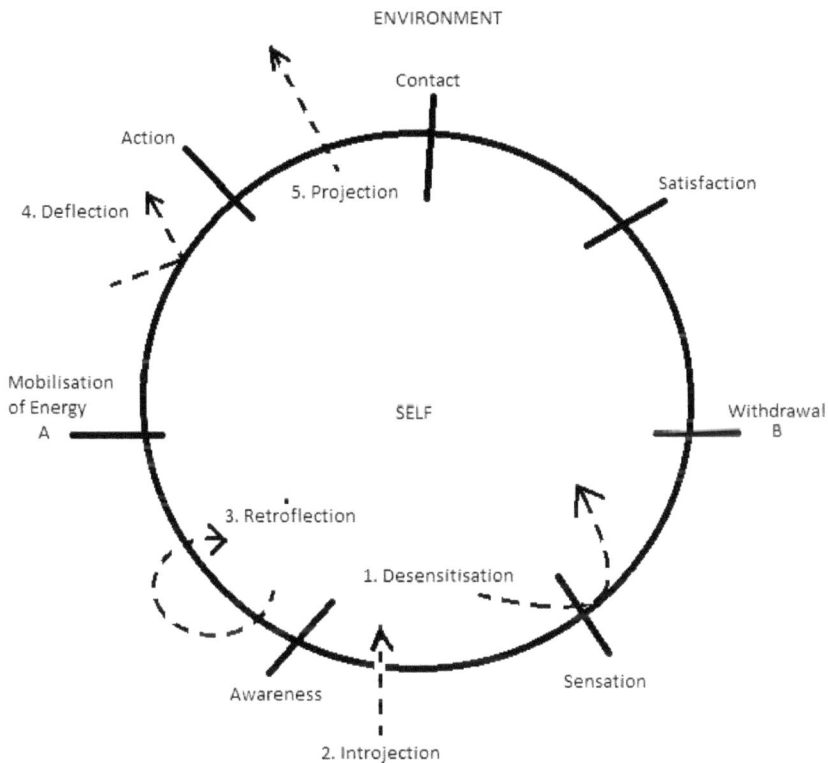

Fig. no. 2. Maintaining of the dysfunctional behaviour

Source: K.Evans, M.Gilbert, 2006, p. 94

The therapist seizes the moment of the client's contact break with himself and the aforementioned mechanisms may be discussed with the client, but there are cases when the mechanisms cannot be discussed, the client's reluctance being too strong. In such situations I consider that the resistance is "eluded" or, more precisely, avoided through a metaphoric language, grace to the Ericksonian interpersonal technique, *by using the Ericksonian intervention patterns*:

- Indirect, open, sufficiently vague suggestions to allow

interpretations, being used to introduce a more specific suggestion oriented towards a particular response;

"You may elaborate a personal, new way of interaction for your particular case";

"and you will preserve what you learn for later moments, you will use it in the days and years to come";

"You will act according to what you learned, starting now".

- The implied suggestions connect something the client is doing to the set therapeutic goal:

"You may discover this time one of the most important significations of your life";

"Before I start to explain it to you, you will feel a state of calmness in your mind".

- Questions or assertions focusing on the conscious or strengthening conscience. Such questions are addressed for the two levels: on the first level, a justified or rhetorical question or assertion is formulated regarding the client's state, i.e. his readiness (relaxation or preparation for hypnosis); and on the second level, the client's response supposes the orientation of the client's attention towards the aspect considered.

"I wonder if you feel ready to start";

"I wonder if, sitting so comfortably and listening to my voice, you have already started to understand what I am saying".

- Truisms are indirect suggestions referring to assertions regarding the human, cultural conditions that are impossible to deny. They are used before the suggestion of a therapeutic attitude we expect to be received with a higher degree of certainty, as they generate an attitude of agreement, of comprehension.

"Each person has a unique modality (to enter a trance, to traverse gestalt, etc)".

- Suggestions covering all the possible alternatives of a class of answers:

"You will be able to enter trance … slowly … gradually … suddenly ... or not at all";
"You will feel relaxation on the level of your face, body, with a sensation of weight ... or release … or not at all".

- The double connection of the conscious / unconscious type allows the therapeutic action between conscious / unconscious. One will recourse to a language which dissociates the conscious from the unconscious, and the client finds out the way instances work.
"On the conscious level – you may not even grasp the moment your unconscious has already started to work in view of finding a solution";
"On your conscious level you may not even seize the moment your unconscious has already started to use your own resources for healing".

- The double dissociated connection of the conscious / unconscious type is an extension of the double connection of the conscious / unconscious type.
"And obviously you may put aside the conscious part to choose the place and moment when you will access what you have learned, assigning your unconscious the task to make it possible or you may let your conscious side learn something and allow your unconscious to select the place and moment when the thing you have learned will be useful for you".

- The reversed conscious / unconscious double connection is applied to the clients reluctant to accept therapy. We involve the client in a struggle, a confrontation mobilising the client's resistance, and thus the attention of the conscious instances are focused on the relation and resistance, and the suggestion will reach the very unconscious.
"It would be good not to relax too soon …".

- The non-contradictory double connection means that one of the suggestive sides indirectly implies the expected answer, and the other part of the suggestion requires the desired answers under direct form. The client has the feeling of freely adopting both alternatives:

"We may start the therapeutic intervention now or we may use the time in a constructive manner";

"You will be able to go in a trance while you listen to me or you will be able to let your conscious state and your sensations get gradually modified …".

b) Break of the contact with the world

The client's defence mechanisms are rooted in introjection (K. Evans), a process by which the client, as a child, absorbed rules, values, attitudes, behaviours of parents, strengthened under the form of punishment and sanction. Consequently, the client's security and well-being depend on the primary care offered by parents. In order to survive, the client, when he was a child, sacrificed himself precisely to adapt to his parents' requirements. The child's sacrifice constituted the fundament of introjection.

Creative adjustment protects the child against the inappropriate parental reality by the shadowing of their own person.

The totality of the messages introjected by the client in childhood constitutes the script of life, defined as a person's intra-psychic process, i.e. "what I think about myself as a person" and "what I think about the world" (see Fig. no. 3; K. Evans & M. Gilbert, 2006, pp. 94-96).

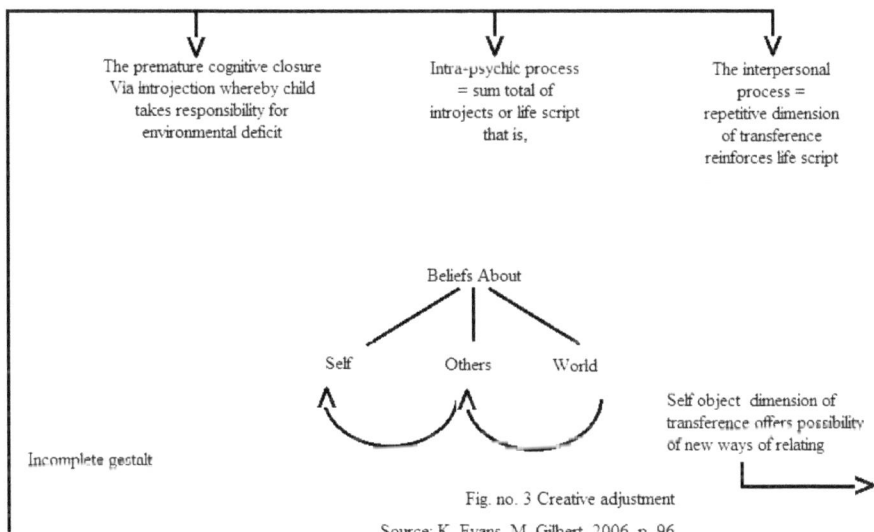

Fig. no. 3 Creative adjustment
Source: K. Evans, M. Gilbert, 2006, p. 96

The intra-psychic structure of a person will influence the nature and qualification of interpersonal relations in order to strengthen the script of life by repetition. The script of life and the pattern of interpersonal functioning influence each other and constitute the basis of relationing, understood by the therapist as being the client's modality to survive "here and now".

Identification with sub-personalities. Techniques in psycho-synthesis

Connection of the K. Evans model with psycho-synthesis

Psycho-synthesis claims that there are two centres in the human psychic, Ego and Self. The Ego is considered a projection of the Self in the conscious zone and it acts as adjuvant on the personality level. The Ego and the Self have a double function, of will and awareness. Psycho-synthesis represents two successive stages, not completely separated however: personal psycho-synthesis and trans-personal psycho-synthesis.

In personal psycho-synthesis, the Ego is the integration core around which the process of personalities' harmonisation and integration takes place, for the person to function effectively in the relation with the environment and to develop an integrated personality.

In trans-personal psycho-synthesis, the focus of the personality integration passes from the Ego to the transpersonal Self; the Ego continues to collaborate in this process, but the transpersonal Self has the major role and becomes the new core around which integration is achieved. Grace to the connection with the transpersonal Self the purpose and significance of life are grasped. The limits of the Ego are overcome by discovering a relation with the universe: a personality cannot be isolated; it is as through it were a part of a larger organism, whose organising core is the transpersonal Self. The therapist helps the client become aware of his own identity and capacity to be liable for his own life, for the path chosen (Drobot, L., *Integrative psychotherapy. Fundaments*, 2009).

The client's childhood creative adjustments through the introjections created (K. Evans) facilitated the identifications with the parent, persons in charge with the child's upbringing, etc, and thus the client's Ego was overlapped, "filled" with the introjected sub-personality (Assagioli).

The client's script of life is in fact the script of the sub-personality with which the client has identified himself, by transfer in the interpersonal relations, as a repetition of the past. Therapy offers an opportunity to "repair the past" by co-creating a mutual therapeutic relationship, a space for the manifestation of the relational development needs and the beliefs about the world, the others, the own Self (the Ego and the transpersonal Self from Assagioli's psycho-synthesis).

In the proposed model, I consider that the therapist's intervention consists in:

- identifying together with the client the introjections the client has done in time;

- identifying together with the client the sub-personalities "played" by the client in the script of life and in the transfers from the interpersonal processes;

- identifying together with the client the beliefs on the world of the Self belonging to the introjected sub-personality.

By changing and discovering the parts played by the introjected sub-personalities, the client has the insight and chance of discovering himself, his own Ego. This is the moment of releasing the blocked energy (Assagioli), activating the client's liberty of decision and action. The aware experience triggers sentiments of elation and liberation. There are situations when the client is afraid of the responsibilities generated by the discovery of his own Ego; in fact, he feels the effect of the repression of the Ego's experiences. Then the therapist reassures him that the parts of his personality he fears help him acquire liberty. I forward as intervention the techniques of Ego strengthening (hypnosis), the hypnosis focused on the symptom, the metaphoric techniques.

I have mentioned that the identifications are done not only with sub-personalities, but also with the emotions and roles the client has played along time. The roles may also be played as central sides or as sub-personalities. A client who identifies herself almost all the time with the role of mother is devastated when the child grows up: she feels she has nothing to live for, as her identification is dependent on the role of mother. As technique in this role identification, the client is requested to play the role of the respective sub-personality by the role game, through the body motions. The voluntary use of identification has the purpose to explore and externalise aspects of the personality that should be better understood.

The identification with certain feelings and emotions allows their release, but first they must be admitted by the client as having been part of him or her before disidentification. Thus, as technique for the disidentification of emotion, the following step-by-step introversion is recommended (Drobot, L., 2005, p. 88):

41

- step I – separating the client from experience in order to become an objective observer. The client's identification with only part of experience does not allow the observation of the whole. For instance, an irritated client (identified with strong irritation emotion) may lose the connection with other aspects of reality such as pain, care, concern, etc.

- step II – the client is asked to focus upon what he feels in that moment of irritation, i.e. to describe what he feels, in what part of the body, what the respective sensations may be associated with, when irritation occurs, how it appears (suddenly, gradually), from what level the client cannot control it any longer, etc.

- step III – the client is requested to represent a situation when he is relaxed, to describe how he feels relaxation, what sensations he loves, what he feels in different parts of the body, etc.

- step IV – the client is required to bring back to memory the way he experiences irritation, to express irritation corporally, by mimic, gestures and then to live relaxation. I ask the client to rapidly traverse the two states, irritation and relaxation, and then ask the client how he feels now that he can "master" irritation so quickly.

By the integration of the Self-Body-Mind-Emotion dimensions, psycho-synthesis makes optimum use of the above dimension. Although the client needs the stabilisation of the physical and emotional sides, he should still understand the patterns and dynamics involved in order to experiment new experiences in his life. The following techniques used in psycho-synthesis are proposed; nonetheless, the therapist's flexibility and creativity allow the application of a vast range of techniques:

- *the empty chair technique* (from gestalt), in which the client may imagine a dialogue with the sub-personality he identifies himself with;
- *the multiple place technique* uses different chairs and pillows

to play different sub-personalities. The client is helped to connect with each sub-personality by dramatic improvisation, symbolic motions, gestures, efforts to become aware of his body. A place is specially set for the "fair witness", the centre, the observer. The centre "speaks" with the sub-personalities involved, helps them understand the dynamics and suggests methods of co-operation. The sub-personalities express themselves freely, manifest fears, resistances, so the centre should answer correctly and encourage them in the beneficial change. The client's central position is a projection of the true central position (of the Self). If the client does not bear the confrontation, the therapist does not insist upon it; the multiple places technique can be reapplied on another occasion.

- *relaxation techniques*, Schultz's autogenous training, the technique (metaphor) of the favourite spot, etc.

At the end, when the second goal (or category of objectives) is reached, one recommends a review, an evaluation of the acquisition acquired by the client in the four domains: behavioural, emotional, cognitive and physiological. The client's progress is encouraged and one recommends the assignment of positive strokes by the client to himself.

From among the techniques for reaching this category of objective one may apply a wide range of techniques, such as: hypnotic, psycho-synthesis, gestalt, relation techniques, etc. In the end, the client is prepared to take another step towards the world; grace to the therapeutic alliance one moves on to the shaping of a satisfying I-You relationship, which constitutes the third large category of objectives set by the therapist.

2.2.3. Objective III (or the third category of objectives). Developing the mutual I-You relationship, solving the problems

Psycho-synthesis continues by the collaboration of the Ego with the transpersonal Self, who assumes the major part; as mentioned, the transpersonal Self becomes the new core of integration. By the connection with the transpersonal Self, one realises the purpose and significance of life, the limits of the Ego are exceeded by the discovery of a relation with the universe. One specifies the fact that not all clients are prepared for the union of the personal will with the transpersonal Self's will. The therapist merely assists the client who wishes to transcend the personal will. As technique, meditation can also be learned and practised on a daily basis. Under no circumstances can the client be forced to reach the transpersonal Self, but all the clients will learn that the change is only theirs and no one from their entourage can be forced to change to their benefit. It is only them who change. Now it is also the time to learn forgiveness and unconditional love. Forgiveness may be understood by analysing the prayer "Our Father", ,"... and forgive us, as we forgive our wrongdoers". However, the client's beliefs will not be attacked by the therapist. The religious affiliation or the absence of religious belief is respected in the therapy practice.

The client has grown up from the viewpoint of his personality, and the bar he was clinging to was and will continue to be for a short while the therapeutic relation. The "It-It" relation (K. Evans) has turned into the "I-You" relationship. Together with the therapist, the client has usually approached his problems and can still approach them, if he so wishes. The indicator, the landmark in the effort of solving his problems, is change. When the purpose is defined by the client his behaviour starts to change as well. The therapeutic approach formulated by De Shazer is realised on the basis of the principle of systemic totality; that is why in this stage it may be advisable to involve the family, but this is not a must. The problem and implicitly the solution can be built so that they could be solved in the interaction system of the client's family. Nevertheless, the framing of the problem must be done in accordance with the client's vision.

The clients share behavioural changes not only on the occasion of evaluation; the seeds of the behavioural change are planted from the very first therapy session. The change must be supported by the therapist because it may be fundamental in finding the solution or solutions to the client's problem or problems. De Shazer conceived several amusing and interesting techniques which are very stimulating for the client in finding the solutions to their problems.

• *the "write, read and burn" technique* – like a ritual, it should be presented with confidence by the therapist to the client. The change from thinking something, writing about it and then burning the note seems an uncertain solution for some clients. The clients who practised the technique mentioned that:

- they have become more concrete in objectivising their thoughts;

- as they had to perform the technique only in a certain period of the day, and at no other hour, the day passed more easily;

- they started to dream about other things, as the "dark thoughts" were no longer forbidden, they were "practised" only in the permitted time span;

- on the metaphoric level, the problems are eliminated together with the smoke resulting from the burning of the papers;

- they found out they had "better things to do".

The technique is useful when the client complains of "obsessive thoughts" or "depressing thoughts". I found that the clients do not write more than four times about their discontentment before discovering they have better things to do.

In the practice, I adapted the write-read-and-burn technique to an even simpler form. I asked the clients to write the most important problems on three pieces of paper, to number them from one (the most important problem), and then to read what they had written and in the end to tear the papers in the sequence corresponding to the order they preferred to get rid of them. It is interesting to remark the clients' effort when they struggled to tear the paper in very small pieces; after they made up a pile of small pieces of paper, I asked the clients to get up and throw them into the garbage bin while also saying, "be careful and don't let any piece of paper escape";

- *the "responsibility of the systematised struggle" technique* – in 1954, De Shazer invented the "responsibility of the systematised struggle", in order to approach the couple issues. The intervention was created for the situation when both partners simultaneously complain about useless fights and quarrels. The ritual involves the following steps:
  1) you flip a coin to decide who goes first (the fight);
  2) the winner has the right to tell all that he thinks for ten minutes;
  3) the other partner then continues, for another ten minutes;
  4) at the end, silence is kept for another ten minutes, and then the cycle is repeated.
  The ritual is not useful when the discontents are high and if only one of the partners complains of the respective thing.
- *the "do something different" technique* was invented by De Shazer in 1978 to fit only a particular situation. The criteria for identifying that particular situation are:

- a person complains about the behaviour of others;

- the person states he has tried "everything possible";

- the person against whom "all possible measures" have been applied reacts in the same manner (annoyingly, obviously).

The therapist recommends: "from now on till the next session do something different, when X reacts (in an annoying manner). Do not care if that action is weird or taken from books; the only thing that matters is that the decision made should be different from the previous ones" (op. cit., p. 123). No specific action is perceived: the client can choose whatever he likes. A slight spontaneous change may generate the solution, but the therapist cannot predict or clarify the client's reaction.

The client is urged to step out of the usual pattern, as change brings the solution. The fundament of the requirement is focused in fact on the client's determination to do something else to attract attention, in order to stop thinking about the problem (discontentment): the therapist usually asks, "So, what else have you done to overcome your temptation in this past week?" This question supposes that something happened, and the client succeeded in overcoming his temptations.

The therapist does not tell the clients exactly what to do differently and does not teach them new techniques. These interventions are discrete, and their impact is extremely important.

As therapist, I ask the client to observe from one session to the next: a theme, the way he behaves at the place of work, in the family, etc, so that he could describe what he wants to happen. I adopted the demand from De Shazer (1984), De Shazer & Molnar (1984b) and it refers to the clients' fixation upon the present and future in order to promote change. The clients expect things to change gradually, and the message formulated showed that the therapist has other expectations: "Important things are already happening, just look". The formulation does not include "if". The message is formulated so that it builds the hopes for change, builds a satisfying prophecy on the future.

I consider the hypno-analytical techniques equally important:
- "Voyage to a rock" (the client in trance "stores" part of his concerns and problems in a safe spot, under lock and key; he can carry his concerns or keep them there, in a safe spot, for a long time);

- "Leaves on the pond" (the client may carefully place his problems and discontentments on the leaves fallen from a tree).

47

Techniques of the Ego strengthening

After the integration of the Ego's sub-personalities by psycho-synthesis, the Ego should be "strengthened". Hypnotherapy has a privileged position compared to other therapies as its arsenal of techniques is unparalleled, but this supposes also the difficulty in classifying its techniques (Dafinoiu, I. & Varga, J. L., 2003, pp. 158-160). Hypnotherapists consider that any psychotherapeutic intervention should be preceded by measures meant to strengthen the clients' sentiment of trust.

In my practice, when I use hypnotic techniques, I am careful to apply the suggestions of Ego strengthening. "The force of the Ego" is operationalised by the self-capacity to put together measures in view of adapting to various life situations, of reaching objectives, of solving the problems so the force of strengthening of the Ego represents "that dimension of self-sentiment that estimates the chances of the person to face different challenges occurred in daily life" (op. cit., p. 158).

P. Hawkins (1993) synthesised several of the most known techniques of Ego strengthening (Dafinoiu, I. & Vargha, J. L., op. cit., pp. 163-164).

- *the photo album technique* supposes inviting the client in trance to imagine an album with all his memories related to previous achievements, moments of joy and happiness, of positive experiences. Then he is asked to open the album on a page from the beginning – age regression – to "live" through all senses of the image so that it might be as vivid as possible and to relive the emotions of that time. After a certain time, the client receives suggestions to return to the present with the positive emotions and to search for solutions for his present problems. Then he is asked to imagine himself in the future, also in the context of the positive emissions associated with the past success, and to project himself to a moment when the problems that are sources of discomfort or pain are already solved and especially to live the satisfaction determined by the reaching of his goals. This image of the future when the problem is already in the past will be "stuck" in the album.

- *metaphors and stories* contribute to the increase of self-confidence, the trust in our own forces and have the role to reach directly the unconscious grace to an appropriate language.

- *positive suggestions* allow the increase of the feeling of personal value and Ego efficiency. P. Hawkins mentions a discrete suggestion formulated by Hartland (*apud* Dafinoiu, I. & Vargha, J. L, op. cit., p. 163): "... with each breath you will feel more confident, more sure of yourself, knowing that you can efficiently deal with your problems, ... and that you can be satisfied with the life you are living ... feeling that you can control in a higher degree all those aspects of your life ... that you consider important – your relations ... your health ... your intimate life – your work ... your family life ... and knowing that all these pleasant comforting feelings ... will continue to become more and more powerful day by day – strengthening even while you sleep, because your unconscious is working for your benefit even then ...".

- *purpose-oriented meditation* determines the strengthening of the self-feeling of the client, by imagining certain scenarios presenting the reaching of final therapeutic objectives. In the same meditation category we can classify the projections into the future (the client imagines himself released from his present problem).

- *the time bridge technique* prepares the client for the confrontation with the problem and for analysis. The technique makes recourse also to the ideomotor signalling, trance induction being preceded by the choice of the fingers corresponding to the "Yes", "No" and "I don't know" responses.

Trance is induced and then the client is invited to evoke a success, a personal achievement (a positive experience) prior to the start of his present problem. One insists on a vivid virtual representation of that memory, on the sentiments of joy, satisfaction, and one underlines that, consciously, the client has many more such memories, and thus he successfully solved the problems on other occasions, felt the same feeling of joy and satisfaction. Those interior resources of the past that helped him so many times will also help him from now on, even if for the moment, at the conscious level, he faces difficulties. The client's unconscious already knows and the client will soon know that he has the resources necessary for solving the problem.

"And when your unconscious knows that it has the inner resources necessary for solving the problem, then the finger Yes will slightly rise".

Then the client is asked to imagine a film or a scene with a certain person, imaginary or real, who is facing a problem similar to his own.

The therapist may continue the intervention identifying the factors responsible for the problem, persistence, identification of the event. Sufficient time is given to the client to live the events on the emotional plane and for the possible spontaneous intuitions.

In the case of a traumatic event, one performs a dissociation from this event, reviewing the events as though they were watching a film (suggesting that it is not the client who lives the event, but another person; the client watches from the spectator's perspective) or the therapist may delay the discussion until the end of trance (or may discuss in trance as well, if the client accepts).

The intervention continues until one identifies all the events responsible for the client's problem, until the client in trance gives the answer YES to the question: "Now that you have seen these things again, can you liberate yourself from the problem?"

After having got the YES answer, the therapist asks the client to imagine the future without the present problem; one insists on the ideomotor signalling, on the confirmation by rising the YES finger; one insist then on the future feelings of well-being "as you feel good now, when you know you can solve this problem and know how good you feel when you know you have solved this problem and know that healing is already under way right now, although you do not realise this yet. And because you will wish to know, probably, the date when you see yourself liberated from the problem you can know that there is a blackboard behind you, like those in school, on which someone has written that date, in white chalk, and if you slowly turn around you will be able to read the date on the blackboard; turn around slowly to see the date ... and when you see it ... your YES finger will slowly rise ... [the therapist now waits for the answer and then continues by saying]: It is OK, now you have found out the date when you will have left behind the problem that is currently bothering you ... and it may be important to know that this date is not the date when you solve your problem but a later date ...".

If the YES answer does not appear immediately, the therapist continues by saying:
"Sometimes the date on the blackboard is unclear, hazy, it takes a little time until it appears perfectly clear ... visible ... you just need to wait a minute for it to become clear ... or you can perhaps raise your hand slightly ... and you can let your unconscious command your hand ... to write slightly in the air ... that date ...

And now, to conclude, your unconscious may receive all that you learned during this session, and when it finishes the YES finger will slightly rise ... It is all right". The technique ends by coming out of the trance.

As mentioned before, there are a great variety of hypnotic techniques. Moreover, to strengthen the Ego one may also use techniques from the Transactional Analysis. In this respect it is useful for the integrative therapist to study 101 T.A. module. I sometimes discuss with the client, when I deem necessary, his positioning within the dramatic triangle (the position of victim,

persecutor or saviour) and the life positions (+ +; + -; - +; - -).
In order to assess the objective (the category of set objectives), I practise together with the client the evaluation of the acquisitions gained on the four planes: cognitive, behavioural, emotional and physiological.

Then I proceed to the client's preparation for his return, with revigorated resources, into the profession and the social environment.

2.2.4. Objective IV (the fourth category of objectives). Professional reintegration

I think that therapy is an opportunity to be acquainted with the professional competencies. Many clients come to therapy because, after a period of absence from the labour market, once returned to work they no longer find themselves (the situation of women returned from the maternity leave). The university graduates experience a professional shock if they succeed in finding a job, as they find a discrepancy between their theoretic training (useless, without benefit) and the practical requirements (the gap between theory and practice is manifest). Another deficit is the absence of professional training adequacy to real professional standards, in accordance with the professional practice. The social and economic problems leave their mark as well in the organisations where people come with the availability to be tolerant, to be confident and patient with newcomers; anxiety becomes a state of facts slowly and steadily. A client who benefited from therapy senses the possible "shocks" of readaptation. The shocks are the situations when the client's Ego forces, resources, learning and change from therapy are validated. This is exactly why the client should be prepared, empowered for professional reintegration. Many a client from therapy is unemployed and in search of a job. Jobs are scarce in a society that blocked for an undetermined period the professional employment interviews. As therapist, I was in the situation to renegotiate the therapeutic contract as the client could not afford to pay any longer. And yet I did not interrupt therapy. The human pain in a therapy practice is a tiny part of the pain outside it. And from this viewpoint I perceive the client as a partner in the great social suffering, except that in the practice we co-create a relationship that remains the guide of interpersonal relationship in the great human pain. It is important that your former client is a guide who co-creates other I-You satisfying relations. There is already more light coming from such lighthouses, and pain is lifted like fog on an autumn morning. The light from the soul comes off only if we want it to. A therapist's flexibility is manifest not only in the domain of techniques, it is proved also in his adaptation to all clients with origins in all social and professional environments; from the little child to the adult over 70, from the unemployed mother with five children, accompanied by the little daughter ("mother does not let you go alone") to the client parking his Audi in front of the practice. Human pain does not select potential clients. And they are all brave because they came to find solutions to their problems and discontentments. Sometimes even the therapist is a landmark for the professional choice of younger clients, who later on become ... psychologists. Let us not forget that in Romania the profession of psychologist is still mixed up with that of psychiatrist.

Evaluation of the professional "balance sheet"
By professional balance sheet we understand a process necessary for the identification of the client's experiences and potentials. Together with the client, one performs a diagnosed evaluation by conducting several personality tests, motivation questionnaires, self-assessment questionnaires (Cădariu, L., 2005).
The assessment instruments used should allow:
○ sketching a profile of competencies;
○ identifying certain domains in which the client may be trained;
○ stimulating the client for his own training, etc.

Assessment instruments
1) Personalised professional project (P.P.P.)
This instrument is an opportunity to set the professional goals, being designed according to the client's aspirations and possibilities. In its

essence, the personalised professional project is a dynamic vision enabling the client to form a strategy of personal development in accordance with his own needs and the organisational needs (if he is employed). In the future, the client appreciates the project as a commitment to himself in his own training.

The personalised professional training is a possible source of competencies for the client and for the organisation. Three stages are delimited in conceiving the project:

a) Analysis and diagnosis of the professional situation

Once the professional problem is identified, one mentions the problems derived from the organisation with reference to the social as well.

Analysis and diagnosis of the problem situation on the different levels, i.e.:		
Individual	Organisational	Social

Table no. 1. Analysis and diagnosis of the problem situation on the three levels.

By means of the problem description, one will analyse on the three levels:

○   identification of dysfunctions, strains derived from the problem;
○   identification of the possible aspects the project may rely on;
○   material, financial, human constraints;
○   basic values guiding the client;
○   perception and best use of organisational culture, of parents, other partner stakeholders, etc.

b) Definition of goals

The definition of goals requires the client and the therapist to clarify them first. The goals are clearly mentioned first, then defined, and will be analysed on the above three levels: individual, organisational and social.

Defining objective on each level, i.e.:		
Individual	**Organisational**	**Social**
O1 ⟶	O1' ⟶	O1"
O2 ⟶	O2' ⟶	O2"
O3 ⟶	O3' ⟶	O3"

Table no. 2. Definition of the objectives on the three levels

The objectives must be realistic, avoid the contradiction with values, mentality, organisational cultural and social values. The incompatibility between objectives, values and culture triggers true tragedies. The client is prevented from avoiding the possible incompatibilities in the future. Consequently, the objectives will be definite, prioritised and ordered in time, also suggesting the future assessment instruments. The client is prepared for the future self-assessment of objectives.

c) Establishment or choice of action strategy or strategies
In this stage one identifies and establishes the resources, methods and means of achieving the project. Grace to the strategy the client shapes his prospective, realistic and correct vision about his reaching the objectives.

Elaboration of action strategies		
Individual	**Organisational**	**Social**
Resources ⟶	⟶	⟶
O1 Means ⟶	⟶	⟶
Methods ⟶	⟶	⟶
On		

Table no. 3. Elaboration of action strategies on the three levels

It is recommended that the therapist stipulates together with the client the signification of the concepts of human resources (definition, place, role); material and informational materials (definitional place, role, etc) so that the personalised professional project might constitute the expression of the dynamics of the client's aspiration level and expectations within the organisation for which he works.

The project is a professional commitment the client assumes and evaluates on his own in the future.

2) The genogramme

The genogramme supposes the representation on the genealogical tree of the professional experiences of ascendants as well as the missions assigned to them and the values transmitted to the client.

By the genogramme the therapist invites the client to draw the genealogical tree of his origin family. The reflection of the client is about work and its representations along generations.

The client is asked to write down for each member of the genogramme (mother, father, maternal grandparents, paternal grandparents, siblings) the date of birth, the date of death if applicable, residence, profession, the professional quality assigned to them by themselves or other persons. Moreover, the client is also asked to formulate for each of the persons on the chart the typical messages regarding work, messages exchanged with the client, messages regarding the importance or disregard of labour, etc.

Finally, the therapist urges the client to formulate a keyword, a quotation, an emblem symbolising the relation between that person and labour for each parental line.

The genogramme is a powerful emotional instrument that strains the client. One may ask questions such as:

- What is and what does the client's social trajectory look like?

- Is the client in a period of continuity or break, of opposition, reproduction of the professional trajectory transmitted by his family and ancestors?

- What is the client's position in relation with the parents' plans?

- What were the professional stakes in the generations prior to the client?
- What is the client's professional patrimony?

3) The biogramme
The biogramme is a useful diagram systematically grasping the connections between the formal and non-formal education, the social and professional activities of the client.

Years	Trainings	Professional experiences	Social experiences	Significant private life experiences

Table no. 4

The client, as he fills in the cells of the biogramme, becomes aware of the connections between his experiences and the events that have marked him.
Like in the case of the previous theoretic objectives, presented in the above category, the therapist has flexibility in the use of the assessment instruments. For the client the journey into the professional life is nothing but beneficial.
As therapist, the instruments presented above are applied to the clients as homework, and their interpretation and discussion are done during the last therapy sessions; the last session is of final evaluation and of ... congratulations to clients on the progress achieved.

Finalising therapy
Sometimes finalising therapy provokes painful feelings for the client.

It is recommended that the therapist encourages the client to express sadness. Not all clients are sad at the end of therapy, but the therapist is attentive to the expression of feelings.

Furthermore, the therapist may receive a negative feedback from the client; but even then the therapist (S. Culley & T. Bond, 2006):

o   helps the client to find another specialist;
o   will analyse himself reflexively in his supervision;
o   formulates a feedback regarding this feeling, feedback presented in a non-critical manner to the client;
o   concretely describes what he supposes has happened;
o   respects the client's rights and choices.

The review of the entire therapeutic process done together with the client is an excellent opportunity to update and compare what the situation was to what it is at present and what can be improved in the future;

o   the therapist recalls the first session;
o   he may play, if the sessions were recorded, some recordings;
o   he discusses with the client the key moment of therapy: the moment of triggering the change perceived by the client, the most painful moment;
o   he discusses the new knowledge acquired and its use in daily life;
o   he discusses the journey through the great categories of objectives;
o   he puts an end to the therapeutic relationship;
o   he reassures the client that the telephone number of the practice will not be changed.

Chapter III

PRACTICAL APPLICATION
LOOK, I AM AWAKE!!

According to the model described in the first two chapters, I analysed the situation of a young woman within a group therapeutic activity. From the therapist's point of view, the four categories of therapeutic objectives have been reached. I point out I have not worked according to the presented model with all the female participants in the group; the hypothesis I had in mind was to validate my own intervention model through a case, in the context of an unstructured group activity. In my experience in the practice I worked with clients in individual therapy according to the therapeutic strategy presented, but I have not worked in this manner before within an activity with an unstructured group. Thus, in my intervention on the client I aimed at the following:

1   Creating and cultivating a thorough empathic therapeutic relation with the client;
2   Identifying the moment when the contact with the client has been broken and implicitly the contact with the world was perturbed; analysing the client's attachment;
3   Identifying the sub-personalities and strengthening the Ego of the client and implicitly of all the group members by various therapeutic methods and techniques;
4   Reinserting the client into the social by cultivating healthy interpersonal relations.

The unstructured group had the role of catalyst, the melting pot for the reconstruction of the client's attachment, as well as the validation of new behavioural models for a better insertion into the social.
Moreover, I set as further objectives:

59

- Analysis of the group participants' behaviour as reflecting mirrors for the Ego of each of them and the implication of these reflections in their behavioural changes;
- Analysis of my own behaviour by practising the "bifocal view". During all the sessions I was concerned with my own behaviour as well, by my transfers and even by the possible counter-transfers.

The group is in itself a kind of small-scale world, but it is a more secure world when old and newly acquired behaviours are practised. The group, through the participants' action, offers:

1. therapeutic strength;
2. behavioural examples, modalities of action enabling the participants to modify their perception;
3. opportunity to provide positive or negative strokes with influence on the participants;
4. conditions for practising the newly-acquired behaviour patterns;
5. behaviour examples for encouraging transfers and counter-transfers among the participants;
6. possibility of feedback for the decisions made by some participants, allowing the playing of certain roles required either by the participants or by the therapist;
7. premises of a culture of assertiveness under the therapist's co-ordination. There are conditions within the group for the development of emotional intelligence and communication skills;
8. therapeutic strength for the therapist as well. ... Certain situations presented by the participants are starting points and opportunities for solving some of the therapist's problems, that the therapist considered already solved;
9. possibility to reconstruct certain dysfunctional attachments for the group participants;
10. possibility of unconditional love and acceptance among the participants in the group, etc.

In the description of the case I had separate meetings with the client and with her permission I included fragments of her diaries. I consider the client is made responsible for his own therapy if involved in certain "actions" with the therapist. Thus, I got the client's acceptance for the publication of the case, I asked for her involvement in different analyses I made, I negotiated the significations of some of her behaviours, I requested her involvement by reading the entire material and "correcting", even completing it. I not only co-created the therapeutic relationship, but I also roughly re-signified her life until now. It is obvious a therapist cannot work in this way with all clients, but the therapist is sure to identify modalities of co-operation with the client in order to "rewrite the script of life".

Case description

The case is about a 33-year-old young woman, client X.Z., who joined the group at the recommendation of another participant. She comes from a family with an "uncertain" past, and she was born prematurely at 6 months weighing only 800 g. She was kept in an incubator for months. The father is unknown, the mother has never revealed her father's identity, and is still keeping it secret. After 3 months she was sent to a hospital home for children in a remote town. The young lady's grandparents were influential persons in the past, their daughter's pregnancy being a big embarrassment and a problem of "deteriorated" social perception. They insisted that their daughter had an abortion when they found out about it, but the pregnancy was recognised too late by their daughter, at almost 6 months, when nothing could be done, especially in a communist era when abortions were forbidden. The close relatives were persons working in the Securitate and although they delayed the identity paperwork for the child as long as they could, hoping that "she will die for sure", the little girl fought for her life in the incubator for months. Because of the premature birth, she was born with a hemi-paresis on the right side, which was super-compensated in time. At present, the client totally uses the left side of the body, but she cannot hear with the right ear and has nystagmus at the right eye, and she wears glasses. Over time, the client graduated from college, she recorded modern music CDs, writes poetry and paints. Until the age of one year and seven months the client stayed in the hospital home, in fact a sort of orphanage. Her mother visited her weekly, taking the train with the money her father gave her. Both the girl's grandmother and mother worked in the same enterprise, but the grandmother had a high position in the communist party. All her mother's attempts to bring her daughter home faced great resistance on the part of her mother, the little girl's grandmother. The young mother tried to obtain a dwelling from the company and, in a meeting when her application was put to the vote, her mother (the little girl's grandmother) voiced her opposition by saying that, "if the girl had a child and does not even know who the father is, she cannot take care of a dwelling either". So the young mother's possibility of getting a dwelling was lost; the family decided to bring the little girl home from the orphanage. Despite all the pressures on the mother, no one could find the father's identity, although the mother knew and still knows it, without revealing it. After a while, the girl's grandmother and mother started to drink, but their vicious quarrels were cautiously hidden. Nevertheless, the grandmother's intoxication became apparent when there were big dinners at home, with "the important persons in the town". The girl was brought home at the age of one year and seven months; the family acquaintances knew she had been with relatives who took very good care of her, where she had peace and quiet. When she was brought home she slept with her grandmother, "Mamma Nuța", until she was 7, when she asked to sleep with her mother. She perceived her natural mother as a friend or a sister; she was her mother's confidant from an early age (so the roles were reversed). She perceived her grandfather as a father-figure, and he took special care of her, being the first to oppose the decision of his daughter to have an abortion. He was known for his faith in God, although he was a high official in the communist hierarchy, and grace to this position he had access to food, connections, money, in a period when Romanians had the right to a ratio of only one litre of oil per month. Both her grandfather and grandmother came from poor families: they were born around 1930-1935. Mamma Nuţa, the client's grandmother, left home with two brothers clinging to her hands at the age of 12 and a half, and ended up hundreds of kilometres away from her family and her native village. Her mother had told her: "No matter what, do not leave your brothers from your grasp". They arrived at another village where three neighbour families took them in. Mamma Nuţa's wish was to stay together with her brothers and so she talked the three "foster" families into letting her bring her mother and father, together with her other three brothers, and accommodate them in the family barn. Consequently, Mamma Nuţa was the binder of her family and by hard work she succeeded in achieving a lot in the long run. Life made Mamma Nuţa's family move from place to place, but then her brothers finished school and were appointed to important positions, while she married "the man of her dreams" and had two twin daughters; unfortunately, one of them died immediately after birth, so she was left with only one child, the mother of my client X.Z. The hardships of life made Mamma Nuţa a strong woman, heavily challenged by hardships, but also confident in the communist ideology: "the communist members are persons who have to sacrifice all for the good of the party", and in time this became a natural state; what was important was the image and what was seen from the outside. My client's mother was gifted from an early age: she was good at drawing, art, theatre, but the follow-up of such a career was not socially desirable, and thus, at around 12, under the attentive guidance of Mamma Nuţa, they cut off their daughter's drawing and ballet classes. At 16, my client's mother took a "severe beating" from Mamma Nuţa: the latter smashed her back against a radiator and fractured her backbone. She was in a hospital for about half a year. The plaster corset worn by Mamma Nuţa's daughter could never be forgotten. The official variant for the hidden tragedy was that the accident took place when the girl was harvesting corn and carried a too heavy sack on her back and broke her backbone (high school students used to take part in farm activities in the communist era). Mamma Nuţa has never admitted the seriousness of the tragedy; she has always claimed that her daughter had deserved the beating. The sick girl (my client's mother) did not graduate from high school with her class; she attended high school evening classes and graduated later, acted in some theatre plays as an amateur, but kept refusing to reveal the name of her child's father, refused to have an abortion and bore her mother's beatings, the insults in the family. Her only silent ally was her father, who even intervened in some key moments. Following the fights with Mamma Nuţa and in the absence of her protective father, the young mother went into labour prematurely and the spontaneous abortion occurred, i.e. my client X.Z. was born. In communist times abortion was forbidden and at the ward door in the hospital there was the Securitate people to find out details about the abortion. The great influence of the family assured a "smooth course of events". The young mother came home without her daughter; the little girl's inclusion into the family took place, as mentioned, at the age of one year and seven months. From my client's memories, her life and her mother's life were supervised by Mamma Nuţa, who systematically ignored the involvement of the natural mother in the girl's decisions. Her talent for art was inherited by my client X.Z. from her mother; as years went by, poetry, drawing and music constituted the inner world of client X.Z. Her questions about her father and even the confusion as regards who her mother actually was marked her evolution. The images with the two drunken women became increasingly frequent, the alcohol abuse became a way of life for my client's mother as well. The years went by, the holidays were spent at a family of some grandparents' friends, but the young grand-daughter was more and more difficult to "handle"; her questions about who her father was were increasingly frequent, and her mother's answers increasingly evasive. She started to sing in a band, she recorded songs and when she was 23 she married a singer from her band 19 years her senior. She was aware that it was not a chance choice. Her decision to get married made her mother and grandmother react negatively. For 9 years she lived in hotel rooms, as they had singing tours all over the country. At the urging of her husband, she started to look for her natural father, whose identity was never revealed to her, although she knew that his identity was not unknown, that her mother was keeping it a secret. More and more tired of searches and fights with her husband, she decided to get a divorce. Half a year after the divorce, she received a phone call from an acquaintance announcing that her former husband had had a fatal accident. Several years after her former husband's death, she remarried and got pregnant twice; each time she had a miscarriage at 5 and 6 months. She wishes to have a child very much. At present she lives with her husband in an apartment. Mamma Nuța is a dedicated churchgoer, and has transferred all her estate to my client; the client's mother is married and lives with her husband, separately from Mamma Nuța.

Several nights before taking part in the first session, my client had a dream. She had found out that I had started to work with a group of clients and asked one client from the new group to ask me if she could join it. Before her participation in her first session, the second in the group activity, the client had a dream. I received the description of that dream as a completion my client considered necessary in explaining her motivation to participate in the group. I did not interpret the dream, but it is suggestive for the client's expectations for her participation in the group.

"23.10.2010; 16.15 hrs
I had some dreams related to my future ...
I was in a glass building, with many storeys, with spiral exterior stairs and interior elevator. There were two former colleagues beside me; they are now gone abroad with their families, they were gone for good. I had had an accident, I was confined to my bed, my sight was also affected ... the room was golden, with cream drapes, solid wooden furniture, mahogany perhaps, and a mirror was masking one corner of the room. The room was on a high floor. The building was mine, was my working space and my residence at the same time, but it was in need of repair. The builders' team were on the ground floor, and I knew I was quarrelling with the foreman, because he wanted to seal the ground floor, justifying that it would be easier to redo the higher floors that way ... (I wonder: must we seal the past, for the future?) a.n.
I told the workers that the ground floor was as important as the

foundation and the building itself ... it should be OK as a whole."

My client's unconscious formulated her expectations for the achievement of the following weeks:

- the transparent glass building may represent the transparency of the group, the desire of each group member to work on a problem ;

- the elevator may symbolise the path the client is ready to take;

- the foreman of the builders' team may be me ... the therapist;

- the building team may be the group colleagues;

- the already anticipated counter-transfer expressed by the quarrel with the foreman, etc.

Description of the case in the context of the group activity

The purpose of the present study is not to analyse the activity of the group, but the case of client X.Z. within the context of the group activity. The action direction with the entire group will be mentioned, but the focus will be on the client. The acceptance for the case publication was obtained both from the client and from the group. The group is heterogeneous, made of clients with college education, of different professions, being an open group, with the possibility of the clients joining or leaving it at will. Receiving new clients into the group is possible only during the first three sessions, to avoid perturbing the group dynamics. I shall proceed by presenting the entire activity of the group session by session; the case of client X.Z. was approached from the perspective of the elaborated integrative therapeutic model, and for the activity of the group I used eclectic intervention methods and techniques from transactional analysis, hypnotherapy, somato-therapy, psychodrama, projective techniques, etc.

Session no. 1

During the first session the group comprised only one male client and several female clients, all the participants being college graduates. The activities started with my introduction, the contracting of confidentiality, general description of the methods and techniques to be applied. In order to "break the ice", I started a story made of two sentences and I continued the story telling with all the clients until each of them continued the story twice. Another theme was each participant's introduction in a few sentences.

The activity went on with the presentation of some charts from the T.A.T., selected by each client, and for 10 minutes the clients had written down on a sheet of paper a story based on the chart. As a result of the stories, of the projections made, I started to work with one of the clients, using the empty chair technique, in a dialogue of the Ego's state and from the perspective of the Transactional Analysis. The consequence for the client was a ventilation of feelings and an emotional catharsis. The session ended with feedback from each client.

Session no. 2

At the scheduled time the group was not in the same composition: two clients were absent. I explained to the group that they are an unstructured group and that their activity will continue even in the absence of the colleagues who were not participating. One of the female clients asked my permission to introduce a new client to the group; in fact, the protagonist of the case study. Her proposal was accepted and, at the following session, a new colleague joined the group. The study will be focused on this very new client, called X.Z.

During session no. 2, the group activity continued with the analysis of different behaviours, practised by the female participants since the previous group session. I encouraged the behaviour identified by the clients as being changed.

As homework for the group activity I worked on the analysis of the injunctions from the transactional analysis; the clients mentioned the dominant injunctions in their life, offered examples since childhood up to the present for the respective injunctions, tried to identify the persons who cultivated their dominant injunctions and how the injunctions were currently acting in their behaviours at present. For the clients it was a session rich in insights.

Session no. 3

The objectives set by the therapist: creating the empathic resonance relation, identifying sub-personalities.

At the scheduled hour, the group started to gather, and one client mentioned that the new colleague X.Z will come, but will be a little late. Each participant occupied their places, but the new client was still missing and was called on the phone. After several Minutes, a young lady appeared, having a well-groomed look, with earpieces in her ears, and she was invited to take a seat in the circle. Without interrupting the group activity, I continued with the stories told by each client about the activities of the previous week

Client X.Z., the subject of the case study, sat down. After a while she stood up, analysed the practice, the flowers, the pictures, looked at each participant, then quietly sat down in her armchair again. After the feedback received from each participant, I invited client X.Z. to introduce herself. The language used was elevated, the client proved to have oratory talent. The client's introductory account was full of humour, metaphors, divagation, poetry lines, because, as she put it, "I have written a lot of poetry"; she has read much literature, and at present she is interested in alternative medicine. While she was speaking, I noticed that several red stains appeared on her neck and chest and I asked her to take off the scarf from around her neck, if she wished to, which she accepted. The client has a stage name and I still asked her what her given name was, and then I grasped the client's dissociation. With her permission I mentioned that I would call her by her given name. In our dialogue I insisted on the dissociation of the client's sub-personalities and I attempted to identify the moment of the contact break with herself; in fact, I wanted to know if the red stains were a consequence of somatisation, of the Ego's attempt to "come" to the surface. I continued with questions about the woman client and not the artist client: how she grew up, where her parents were, how she passed through life. Then I found out she was prematurely born at 6 months, her father was unknown, she was in an orphanage and all the women who took care of her were "Mom A; mom B ...". At the age of one year and 7 months her "biological mother" took her home. I issued the hypothesis of a continual perturbed attachment in her attitude towards herself as well, the manifestation of at least two sub-personalities with special focus on the "artist sub-personality", willing to be refusing to be herself. The attempt to "reconcile sub-personalities" was done in time by poetry writing, as a silent cry of seeking the lost attachment. I asked the client to put her hand on her chest and to continue to speak, but maintain the contact with herself and to use the syntagm "I-X.Z." when she spoke about herself, without using the stage name. I remarked that the stains were beginning to disappear, and I also made the indirect suggestion, "*I am sure that until next week the stains will disappear*". Indeed they did and have never reappeared in the days and months since.

For the entire group I applied a naturalist induction, before the end of the session. I considered the trance opportune, and the relation of empathic resonance was realised with each client from the group. Here is the trance I applied:

"You are resting on the chair ... eyes closed – comfortably seated ... you may even notice how ... from time to time ... your eyes seem to want to open ... and this is very good ... because I would not want you to go into a trance ... to relax ... too soon. It is much easier.... or rather ... it will be much easier ... to let develop ... to feel that sensation from the shoulder ... or from a hand ... or from the back of your neck ... from the arm ... or from the leg ... while you continue to listen to my voice ... while you hear the sounds of the room ... and

the outside sounds ... from other rooms, ... while you relax ... and in time you are very attentive to the modification of the sensations from the shoulder ... arm ... hand ... back of the neck ... leg ... and you wonder if you will be able to go into a trance ... to relax ... your conscience has already started to let itself be carried ... plunge into time ... and you are letting your body relax ... and you are letting your thoughts ... relax ... together with your body ... being without knowing for the moment ... so much the better ... and so much the more comfortably ... you may feel ... Each of us ... lived faster... or slower... the experience of falling asleep in front of the TV ... when we were trying to follow the action on the screen attentively ... closing our eyes only for one moment ... to rest them ... and listening to the music ... continuing to listen to the voices ... sitting like that ... comfortably and relaxedly sitting ... when a word or a line ... or a sound ... would evoke a certain memory ... and you are going under ... [...] and dreaming for some time [...] and coming back to earth ... and plunging again ... and dreaming again ... until the words and the music merge into a quieting sound ... in an acoustic background ... for thoughts ... for dreaming ... while your unconscious continues to hear ... all that I am about to tell you ... because you have always known ... how easy it is to learn something ... to understand something ... when you are relaxed ... although I do not want you to relax too profoundly from the very beginning ... because ... for the moment ... it is much more important for you to recognise the small changes ... those minuscule modifications ... barely observable ... from your breath ... from your pulse ... those modifications found in the face relaxation ... in the sensation of comfort ... and of security ... that is enveloping you ... and your unconscious may wish ... to relax your small finger ... before that sensation occurs in your thumb ... or maybe of your unconscious ... your wrist ... will be the most appropriate place to start relaxation ... while your unconscious may savour the curiosity related to the question where exactly these sensations will appear first ... sensations of relaxation ... of détente ...

When you throw a pebble into a lake ... on the water surface concentric rings will quickly spread ... but, exactly underneath the

70

water ... under the surface of the conscious ... the pebble will go down ... gradually and while it is going down ... passing by the beings ... who live in the water ... while it is immersing ... passing by the vegetation living in the water ... slipping slowly ... slightly ... nothing will be disturbed around it ... when it slightly sets at the bottom of the quiet lake ... and ... gradually ... even the rings on the water will quiet down ... and underneath the water everything becomes calm ... quiet again ... and you may yourself recognise the capacity ... to meditate comfortably ... somehow ... to the problems that trouble you ... You remember those times ... when you were sure that things were in a certain way ... and suddenly you realised that they had changed ... had modified ... had become something totally different ... like the times when you were a child ... and discovered that the lamp was the lamp ... or were learning the difference between house and table ... changing what you had thought before for what you were learning then ... with new meanings ... new modalities to act ... and I wonder if these new sensations ... if these hypnotic sensations ... related to relaxation ... will remain the same ... unchanged ... if they will continue to deepen ... while now you are trying to remember everything I have told you ... about these dreams in front of the TV ... about those pebbles ... going deeper into the lake ... sometimes more rapidly ... sometimes slower ... about those childhood memories ... connected to things that seem to be something ... and turn into something else ... about meaning ... sensations ... that change ... sometimes faster ... some later on ...

And now... when your unconscious will allow your conscious ... more and more ... to take cognisance of sounds ... of my voice ... of the sounds in this room ... of the sensation you feel in your arms ... legs ... of the variety of thoughts and feelings flooding your ... your conscious comes again to the surface ... gradually ... and you are gradually returning to the state of conscious vigil ... and everything is all right ... your eyes are opening ... that's it ... to the state of conscious vigil ... you are entirely returning now ..."

I invited the group to a meeting organised during the following week, at the university where I teach, a meeting with Peter J. Hawkins and

Richard Page. At that conference all the group was present, including the client, and she was very interested in the topics approached, and at the end of the conference she wanted to have a picture taken with me and Peter. I think that both her sub-personalities were present in the photograph, sub-personalities identified in the previous session. For client X.Z. the "ground floor restoration" began, like in the dream, after the client read at the end of therapy the material sent by the therapist, and she added the following:

"12.11.2010. 17.00 hrs
progress report
1- reminder of the set goals
- re-directing of vital energy
- re-programming
- re-union
- re-discovery
2 my mom ... [in English in original, without corrections]
broken down in agony,
wonderin whats left of me
fit the pieces in the puzzle ... why am I to solve the problem?
am I better? am I stronger? four leaf clover?
is the time to turn the page , am I now the chosen age?
soul and mind and body ... strange ... am I closer or just fallin
what exactly is my calling ... and to whom I choose to listen
caught in sweet deceiving wisdom
for my signs I light a candle, for my Lord, I praise, not gamble
I'm crawling back into the cradle" [end of fragment in English in original, without corrections]

"A(ici) (acu)M (here and now)   20.11.2010
For Maria (the painter)
I thought the wound has closed, but it sill hurts and I realise
That instead of healing ... it is spreading ... growing bigger ...
And from the body is clinging to the soul ... and from the heart to the mind ...
Instead of prayer there is only howl ... if she loves, why is she lying?

The cry in the night takes me to the stars and throws me ... and lets me ... find the way home
It still hurts, I am still longing ... but I put on my mask, and I die again,
I crawl and although it hurts, I want my Father's Forgiveness
● *the father, here the Heavenly Father ..."*

It is possible that the client, unconsciously, by accepting to participate in the activity of a group, should have foreseen the "reopening of wounds". In the group activity one brought to the surface of the conscious the somatisation, two sub-personalities, they were brought to the surface and "stood face to face". The client mentioned she could better express herself in English, she could be more easily extrovert, and she "felt released" if she spoke her mind in English. She learned English all by herself; as a child she received a book and started to read, to learn the alphabet, but the particular book was a course-book for English. ... Two languages, two sub-personalities; in every-day life the Romanian speaking sub-personality is expressed, and when she writes poems and sings she expresses herself in English (with a stage-name).

Session no. 4

Therapeutic objective: analysis of the broken contact with the Self and the world, attachment approach.

I had established in the previous session that there was a perturbed attachment of my client to her mother and to the world. Once the perturbed attachment is brought up, it will lead to the moment of the client's contact rupture with herself and with the world. As therapist, I had to avoid the possible resistances put in motion by the client and to maintain the identified sub-personalities on the plane of conscience at the same time. In the group there was a client who had a perturbed attachment to her daughter. I considered that by approaching the attachment at the respective client, by role-play, I would offer directions of analysis for client X.Z. as well.

At the scheduled time, the group arrived; client X.Z. was only a few minutes late. In the first part of the session, after the feedback from each member of the group about the previous week's news, I worked on the dysfunctional relation between one of the female clients and her daughter. I staged a role-play, after a telephone conversion with her daughter, described by the client. I cast client X.Z. in the role of the other client's daughter, in order to ask for help in a problem. I recommended the part to client X.Z. to bring forward her relationship with her mother. The scene was interpreted and later on I asked my clients to change chairs and to play the parts in reverse (the daughter to sit on the chair where the mother sat and vice versa) and then they returned to their places. I continued the role-play with my involvement and the participation of another client from the group; we went to stand behind the two clients (mother and daughter) and I played the role of the daughter's "conscious but un-verbalised voice", and another client from the group played the part of the mother's "conscious but un-verbalised voice". The dialogue and the role-play was therapeutic for all three clients. A pause was taken, and then the clients' feelings were examined with the highlighting of the realities of each. I used the role-play to avoid the client's resistance and for client X.Z. it was a delicate modality to admit the needs of the sub-personality were "enabled" to come to the surface; there was the risk of the sub-personality being smothered at any time, and for the somatisations to reappear.

Client X.Z. brought three photo albums to show herself (going by the given name) in different moments of her life. From her account I realised her joy in reliving the contact with herself, contact she starts to take care of, bit by bit. By means of photos she was trying to identify herself, i.e. X.Z. and not the artist sub-personality. The stains disappeared and have never reoccurred since the previous session; when she was speaking about herself she used to take her right hand to her chest and mentioned that all week she took care of herself, she was attentive to insights, to dreams. She also brought a poetry notebook. I listened to a song on a CD; and she had an insight that her verses were the symbolic expression of seeking her lost attachment to herself. Then I suggested the client identify examples of situations when she wished to search for the lost attachment with herself in all and everything. After a short moment of thinking, she remembered the visit she made to the maternity ward in Reşiţa, the ward of the HIV-infected children, when she was 16. Then she took all the children in her arms, one by one (when she was talking about this, she took off her glasses). On the occasion of the same visit, she remembered a little boy aged one who was stretching his little hands towards her through the bars of the bed. The image of that little boy haunted her for a long time. I asked her how old she thought she was, emotionally, when she spoke about memories, and she answered, "*I feel twelve or fourteen years old*". I encouraged her, pointing out that in the weeks to come she would grow up emotionally.

I asked her if she had dreamt anything in particular, if she remembered a dream from the previous week since the previous session with the group. The client made the account of her dreams in verses:

> "*The unseen demon – from waist down –*
> *As though separated from me, repulsive, curiously hideous*
> *And still part of me ...*
> *I am saying the prayer, he is laughing and defying me ...*
> *I end by saying – Ana-maria*
> *And look, I am awake ...*"

After having listened to the verses written by the client, I told a metaphor, stating that each of us has two wolves inside ourselves, one white and one black; it depends on us, on each of us, which wolf we choose to feed in different moments of our life. Then she showed the group photos from different periods of her life. She mentioned that every day she remembered a sequence from childhood and then consciously she would take her hand to her chest to connect with herself. Near the end of the session I asked for her consent to write about her case and the agreement of the group to record with the future session. I got their consent and the client's approval to write and publish certain aspects of the group activity.

I offered the group a positive stroke and I thanked them all for the manner in which they co-operated within the group.
At the end of the session I applied the "rainbow" metaphor:

"Sit down as comfortably as possible ... on the chair ... in the armchair ... breath in deeply ... keep the air deep inside ... for a few seconds ... and now ... as you are slowly breathing out ... let your eyelids close ... And as you are sitting like that ... comfortably seated ... breath in deeply and quietly ... and imagine your favourite cloud ... a large ... white ... puffy cloud ... descending slowly ... slightly ... beside you ... so close that you can climb on it ... you can embark on an imaginary journey ... you can feel its softness ...and the delicate support ... the cloud is offering you as it envelops you ... and as the cloud is slowly ... slightly ... rising ... you feel yourself floating ... you are floating, climbing to the sky ... comfortably seated ... protected ... completely safe ... And while the cloud is slowly rising ... slightly sliding to the sky ... a little playful bird ... is coming down to you ... and is standing on your cloud ... beside you ... it is looking at you inquisitively ... with its tiny ... shiny eyes ...as though it were inviting you to follow it ... to play with it ... And now it is spreading out its wings ... it is folding them again ... it is taking off ... rising and descending, playfully flying around the cloud ... letting itself be caught in a warm air current ... completely free ... taken by a light breeze ... and your cloud seems to wish to follow the bird ... while you are wondering ... where it could take you ...

Looking down ... you can see underneath ... the trees' canopy ... and ... surprisingly ... from here ... comfortably seated on the cloud ... you can see so well ... so clearly ... each branch ... each twig – each leaf ... contoured in delicate lines ... and you can see ... equally clearly and well ... the green hills ... the golden wheat crops ...rocking ... back and forth ... in the wind ...
Now you notice ... the golden ribbon of a creek ... winding its way towards the valley ... its surface reflecting the blue sky ... and the sunshine – And now ... you can see a rainbow at the horizon ... you can see it very clearly ... arching high in the sky ... It seems the bird

has also seen it ... and now it has decided ... to fly towards the rainbow ... And you are closing in ... you are wondering at the effervescence of the rainbow colours ... each colour ... is so bright ... as if covered in silver drops ... sparkling in the light ... and giving it such a special ... shine ... You are fascinated ... by the playful shine of colours ... these colours don't resemble ... anything you have seen before ... And the bird ... is taking you first ... into a splendid light ... of an ivory pink ... It is the delicate ... colour of fresh dawn ... enveloping nature ... coming to life ... It is as though ... you yourself were offered ... a new way of waking up ... the chance of a new beginning ... and everything around you ... including the cloud carrying you ... is reflecting the pastel shades ... covering you ... while the ivory colour ... is gradually turning ... into an orange-blue ... delicate ... like the shine of the sky ... before sunrise ... It is the colour ... that brings ... the promise of healing warmth ... of sunlight ... You are walking into this colour ... and feeling health ... spreading through your whole being ...

And now you see ... how the little bird ... is taking you ... to a shady place ... fresh and green ... a green symbolising growth ... renewal ... such a wonderful colour ... so full of possibilities ... It is the colour of spring ... of young ... fresh ... plants ... of leaves sprung from the buds grown on the winter's grey branches ... carrying the love ... that colour we all wait for ... since the moment the dark cold winter days ... begin to grow ... It is the colour that lights us ... and cheers us up ... bringing the promise of a new spring ... And from here ... you let yourself be carried to the clear blue sky ... You don't know any longer ... if it is the playful bird ... or your imagination ... that is fully savouring this colour ... this colour blue ... bringing calmness ... serenity ... peace ... and comfort ... Gradually ... the blue starts to turn ... into the soft crimson of sunset ... a very appropriate period for contemplation ... for reviewing ... for reassessment. An opportunity ... to acquire a new meaning in life ... in the universe ... You may see ... the little bird ... with its shiny feathers ... floating about through the colours of the rainbow ... as if it were making you a sign ... inviting you ... or reminding you ... that you yourself can be a part of this universe ...

77

And deep down ... inside you ... you know that now the time has come ... to come back home ... to let your favourite cloud slide ... float away ... to the place where this journey started ... to remake the way you took together ... accompanied on this journey back ... by the small bird ... which is playfully rising and descending around it ... around you ... sending you a sign ... inviting you to play once again ... but you know that the time to play is over ... for now ..,...and that the cloud on which you continue to sit comfortably .. will carry you back ... completely safely ... bringing you back here ... into this room. Seating you again in the chair or armchair you left behind ... And thus ... you are returning to your conscious side ... becoming again perfectly awake ... knowing that you can meet again ... whenever you wish to ... your favourite cloud and the guiding tiny bird ... and the rainbow in the distance ... And knowing it ... you will be able to let your eyelids open slightly ... slowly.

Client X.Z. is more and more prepared for the journey into her inner depth. She was guessing that painful themes were about to be touched, for which she herself has attempted to find interpretations during her life. The therapeutic relationship is more and more solid, the group better and better bound. When she read the material, the client considered it important to add the following diary entries, considered significant:

"23.11.2010, 04.15 hrs
It is almost 2 years since I had my first miscarriage.
How many times I wonder do I have to receive the lesson of loss, before I become a mother? Where have I gone wrong? What is it I don't understand yet? OK, I already know that I wanted to become a mother, the artist in me was not very willing ... but now that I have realised it, is it enough? Or are there more details, or other Egos out of my reach? Only after I lost my first pregnancy, grandmother became aware I was a woman ... my pain made her understand it ... has she seen herself maybe? Since then I can have adult to adult conversations with her. Mother was also beside me ... like a friend who also understands what I am going through ... because she as well has been taught the lesson of loss ...

78

The lesson of loss or only a recreation, a rebirth of mine, a memory of the way I came into this world ... alone ... against everybody. I was just a child ... how could I have a baby, before I myself ... became a Woman?

24.11.2010, in the morning ...
I had a very confusing dream ... I took from it what I felt to be the message sent ... now, how and why and from where and in what way, the guilt feeling from my unconscious/or before birth, this meaning projections, thoughts, states lived by my mother when the child was still in her womb, perceived by the foetus thus has direct implications in the conscious."

As therapist, I did not know what the client was thinking and doing between two group sessions, but after having read the text addendums and having reviewed the content of our following sessions, I realised that unconsciously the client was anticipating the therapeutic process, i.e. the approach of the moment of the contact break with the world. By resignifying the attachment to her mother, to herself (putting her in contact with herself, the self-acceptance) it was obvious that some interactions were bound to change on the relational plane; but even I as therapist was guessing that it was possible to reach the moment of the contact break with the "world". The deepening of the theoretic approach had to be done with great caution, because:

- it was necessary that the client be empowered in maintaining and accepting the contact with herself (by accepting her "given name" sub-personality, the practice of that sub-personality in daily life a calm relationing with her volcanic sub-personality exhibited on the stage);
- the historical diagnosis was loaded and overwhelming; the client has done a lot of searching to soothe herself. Many of her quests have received certain labels from her part and others were left "at the will of the Heavenly Father" (I do not know my father, but I still got one, the Lord). The failure of sub-personalities' reconsideration

- the client was "uncovered" before me as therapist and I was risking losing the relation of empathic resonance if she were to bring too much load from the inside of her unconscious. I thus considered it necessary to work with the entire group through techniques for the Ego strengthening. I consider that the explanation of the Ego's states from the Transactional Analysis involves any client in his or her self-analysis.

Session no. 5 Therapeutic objective: strengthening the ego and sub-personalities

There was another client in the group, a college graduate, employed as a secretary at one of the faculties of our town's University. Two years ago, the client's father died, leaving behind a family with high debts, with firms that were closed and creditors who were threateningly asking for their money back. The remaining family, the client, had had no prior knowledge about the financial troubles of the firm, and after the father's death the problems surfaced even before his funeral. In the following months the client lost her hearing, she underwent four surgeries, the right-ear hearing apparatus was totally removed, and she has only half of the left-ear internal apparatus left. Thus, the client is diagnosed with medium to severe hypoacusy, and from the psychological viewpoint she has very low self-esteem, feelings of uselessness, of being a burden to the family (the client is divorced, she has an 18-year-old son in her care and her mother is diagnosed with cancer).

At the scheduled time, client X.Z. arrived on the dot, and I congratulated her on being so punctual. X.Z. was open to dialogue and asked for my permission to have a cup of coffee: *"What if you hypnotise me today? May I have my cup of coffee first?"*. Her tendency to show off made her announce to her "biological" mother that she was a "case study for me". I remarked that she had simply called her biological mother Maria, her actual name. In order to continue with the integration of the client's sub-personalities, I asked her to give some feedback to the hypoacusic client. Thus, client X.Z. sat in front of her, took her hands and encouraged her in the process or actualisation, told her that she herself could not hear at all with one ear, that she could not see very well, that although she had very accented astigmatism she sang, she was currently taking driving lessons, and continuing her life by all sort of activities. The participants in the group offered positive strokes, both to client X.Z. and to the hypoacusic client. The group activity continued, but at a certain moment client X.Z. searched for crayons and sheets of paper and drew varied sketches and an athematic drawing which she gave to the hypoacusic client at the end of the session. I encouraged thus the transfer between the two clients, I allowed the manifestation of Free Child in client X.Z. What was also interesting was the client's sitting next to me, at my desk, like a child quietly doing her homework, but who in fact is everywhere in the practice. For the group I prepared the debate of some topics from the Transactional Analysis: analysis of the Ego states, the dramatic triangle and the winner's triangle, as well as the analysis of life positions. Each client had something to say about the insights from the inspection of daily life. Client X.Z. was putting down the information she considered important, interrupting her drawing whenever she wanted. If she had something to say, she tried not to divagate from the subject, which should be appreciated, as she herself identified with the Romanian actor Florin Piersic in her manner of speech …

In the above session, from the perspective of the integrative therapeutic model, I activated the sub-personality of client X.Z., that side of the client who has hypoacusic issues, sight problems, aspects that had always been hidden or well masked in the interpersonal relations. From the viewpoint of the Transactional Analysis, the states of child ego, adapted child interacted for both clients. I asked the clients to change places and to formulate strokes from the new positions. The exchanges of messages, of roles between the two clients, after changing places when they were exchanging the messages, facilitated the bringing to the surface of sub-personalities. The client with medium hypoacusy by identification with client X.Z. activated much sooner the psychological processes necessary for a better integration and adaptation to the social; whereas client X.Z. entirely expressed the state of the child Ego. For client X.Z., the session was therapeutic grace to her putting to high value and acceptance of her behaviours, with the mention that "bit by bit, I started to grow emotionally".

All participants worked hard when the dramatic triangle and the winner's triangle were presented. The session ended by setting up the next meeting.

When she read the materials, the client added the following text (*in English in original, without corrections*):

"another night, another dream
I was suposed to clean up my bedroom ... and guess what I found under my bed ... my mother-in-law's balerina shoes, a broken baby chair ... so, I told my husband we must clean-up this mess, that his mom left behind ... oh, also the door from our bedroom was broken, ..., he said that he doesnt need to clean up that mess, that he'd rather just leave everything as it is, as long as it is underneath, not shown, its not a problem for him ... the landscape changed and I was in my grandma's house, doin' the same thing, cleanin'.
I was throwin' away the dolls ..." (*end of the fragment in English in original, without corrections*).

Session no. 6. Identifying the break of contact with the world and bringing the dramatic content to the surface

The participants in the group continued the analyses of their important interpersonal relations in their life from the perspective of the dramatic triangle, and their insights helped them understand the significance of certain behaviours practised in the past but also at present.

The hypoacusic client had a week of well-being; the change for the better was remarked on and appreciated by her mother and son. She also described something that occurred at her place of work: together with a co-worker, she took some documents to a higher department and asked one of the secretaries to speak louder. The colleague who was with her mentioned as an "explanation" that "she does not hear, she is deaf". The client, very firmly, replied, "I am not deaf, I am hypoacusic". When she was back in her office, she congratulated herself on her answer; she enjoyed self-contentment, the courage she had proved: "*I felt like I have not felt in a long while*". Another client made some changes to her exterior look: she had her hair cut and dressed well, and underlined that, "*This is the way I used to be, now I seem to be afraid of well-being*". I replied, "*I gather that you have turned from victim to winner and you are afraid. How does a winner behave?*". I addressed this to all participants in the group, asking them to offer feedback to their colleague, a positive stroke, the client being at the centre of the group with the request to thank everyone for their input. The positive appreciations came very fast and the client was happier and happier with what she was receiving. She succeeded in eliminating some of the fears to be highly valued and especially she began to learn how to receive messages from the others.

Client X.Z. was attentive to the accounts, offered the required feedback and in the current session I allotted the remaining time to the therapeutic labour with her. I considered the group to be strong enough to have the necessary therapeutic resources to cope with what was coming next. As therapist, I am always careful not to offer, not to urge, the client to make insights more than he or she can receive at that moment. I attempt to manage as efficiently and comfortably for the client what is called in education the zone of proximal development: what the client learns should strain him or her only a little more than he or she has already offered. Each pupil can learn everything, but it all depends on how the teacher presents the information; it is the same with clients: they are developing at their personal pace, and it is up to the therapist what and how much he or she is engaging the client in the lessons about her or his own ego. I initiated a dialogue with client X.Z.

"How old are you now?
I am about 17.
Do you want to have an analysis of the important events in your life from birth to the age of 17?
Yes.
What significant things happened to you until the age of 10?
Many things.
How did you manage to cope with the events with more or less pleasant impact on your life?
By means of drawing, poetry and singing.
Where shall we start your account?
Well, I was almost four and I had anaemia. My grandparents used to send me to spend my holidays with a family near the town X. They were about 50-60 years old. I was in the middle of nature there; I would stay with that family, they were paid to have me. The lady was rather ill and we went together to Baile Herculane Spa, where they received some treatments. I remember that the man started to talk to me about women, about what men and women do together. I did not understand some of the words; I had never heard them before. I. kept spending my holidays with them; I was seven and I remember that he would come into my room, stood before me and masturbated. I was looking through him, wishing for it all to end as soon as possible. He made me promise that when I became a woman after my first cycle I would have sex with him, take care of him and love him. A woman

84

must not refuse a man when he wants to have sex, as this harms him; women attract men and they are guilty for this attraction. This is what I heard every Saturday evening and on Sunday morning I went to church with them. He was the first to sit in the pew. I used to stare at a Saint Virgin Mary icon and pray. I kept wondering if there was something wrong or not. I felt it was not all right, but, on the other hand, if he came to church and prayed, was respected ... I talked to no one about this; I did not know how to put it. I would crouch in a corner of the bed, he was before me ... He came into my room at night, sat beside me, touched me, I was petrified ... I wished for it all to end as quickly as possible. When I grew a little older, I refused to got to them. But my grandparents still sent me. When I was ten or eleven, one winter, I went to them again. I knew I was about to have my first period, and I was afraid of what was to come. In the morning I went to the garden and I saw the stained underwear, then wrapped myself in a couple of toilet paper rolls. I put my ski costume over the clothes and we all went to church. I saw the icon of Saint Virgin Mary near the entrance and I knelt. I don't remember what I did. A woman saw me and called the man's wife. I felt and heard nothing; when they picked me up I was stained with blood all over. I shouted at the top of my voice that I wanted my mother to come and take me home; she did, and the same afternoon we returned home to Reşiţa. Since then, I keep shuddering when someone touches me. I remember that another year I went to that family with grandpa and I spent the night, and I slept in grandfather's bed. In fact, I did not sleep at all; I was afraid not to excite grandpa. I attempted to silence even my breath ... When I was 17, one holiday mother wanted us to go visit them, as we had not seen them for several years and they missed me – They kept asking why I had stopped visiting them. I would come up with all sorts of explanations to avoid going there. I used to dress in black; I did not show I was a woman, so that I did not provoke anyone ... But we still went, and although I was reluctant, we had to stay overnight. I watched the last bus leaving and I remained with mother. I went to the backyard, but he came after me and started to tell met that I had to have sex with him, although I had already started my sexual life. I had to sleep with him, as I had promised that I would love him. He grabbed me by the hand and I began to shout at him that if he did not let me go I would kill him. His grasp was still strong, and I was still afraid of him. We left the following day and I have not seen him since. I heard he came to Reşiţa to look for me; he is ill now, confined to his bed and insists on seeing me. I don't want to see him ever again ..."

The whole group was petrified. I rose from my chair and I sat beside client X.Z. She had started to cry and I asked her if she wanted us to continue, and she said yes. I began with a naturalist induction, focused on the breathing pace, with the suggestion to keep her right hand on her chest to be in permanent contact with herself and I made a hypnotic regression until the moment she stood petrified in the church, at the age of 10-11, and in the trance I offered suggestions regarding her womanhood, the acceptance of her femininity that she had attempted to reject all these years. In fact, I focused on the age span from 10 to 17 or18 years. I also offered suggestions to the unconscious to access resources *"from now on, in the moments, hours, and days to come ... whenever our conscious needs it ..."*. The client continued to weep; she kept her eyes closed, in trance, and I raised her from the chair, hugged her and talked to the 10-year-old girl. With calmness, I soothed her and I reassured her that no one was going to abandon her ever again, that it was OK for her to grow up in full safety as a woman, to accept herself, that she could take care of herself without problems, addressing thus to the adult as well. From gestalt I know that touching the client is advisable only in certain circumstances, otherwise one risks strengthening the dysfunctional gestalt cycle by touching or caressing; the client had been sexually abused, and it is obvious the aggressor started by touching, caressing, hugging her, etc. She stood there crying for minutes. I sat her back in her chair and I performed the return from the trance and not only: the lost attachment to herself was rebuilt. All that time the group was an active spectator for the client, but also for each and every one of them: I remarked on the fact that all the female clients had tears in their eyes.

I shall attempt to approach regression from the gestalt perspective, in order to describe the therapeutic intervention. The client has an artist personality, the body language is her main "introduction card", the way she moves, comes closer, gets away. The client's entire body enacts her feelings, needs and beliefs. For most clients, it is extremely important to become aware of what was avoided, discarded. In the case of the client, femininity was put aside, even maternity, when she wished to be a mother, but paradoxically she denied what being a mother meant. The client had to reconnect with the energy, vitality and intelligence of the corporal processes: "restoring those natural processes may be a major factor for healing and re establishment of the person's functioning as a whole" (P. Joyce & C. Sills, 2001, p. 249). I started the client's process of reconnection with herself from the very first session:

- becoming aware of her own body, both by underlining the visible stains on her chest, and my request to remove her scarf from around her neck;

- I developed a relation of the client with her body with the help of syntagms like: "I feel a tension in the chest area";

- changing her breathing patterns, with focus on her own breathing. Sometimes the mere attention upon breath may be transforming for the client;

- the client's harmonisation with herself by touching her chest with her hand. So I did not practise touching from the first session; her touching her chest with her own hand continued during all the following weeks, whenever it was necessary.

My touching and hugging the client after three more sessions in the regression performed had the role of giving support to the client, to reassure her before her troubling emotions and obviously to prove my empathy. The client was regressed to a certain age and, when I took her in my arms, she did a strong paternal counter-transfer, and to avoid any possible destabilising effect, I returned the client to an adult relationship by means of the suggestions offered in her state of trance. I worked with the phenomenological interrogation after the client came out of her trance: when, here and now, and I asked her to think about her experience. The client did not become "younger", she merely expressed an aspect of her personality as a whole; the client was regressed, but she has permanently a non-regressed self, with various degrees of accessibility and awareness: "regression ... may be regarded as an activation by the individual of a previous level of development, while the next level, at least for a while, is abandoned" (Staemmler, 1997, p. 52).

What was therapeutic for the clients in the group was the fact that they realised another side of human suffering, its depth, and thus the problems of some of the clients began to seem, as one client put it, "*syrup in cold water*". In order to support the client's comprehension of some of her behaviours, I offered possible interpretations to her "child-like" actions. All those manifestations were nothing but hidden forms of a hurt-suffering child, who kept doing all sorts of activities like a cheerful child, the adult behaviours being rare. The state of joyous child "to whom you could not resist" was the covering "mask" for a wounded little girl, afraid of what being a woman meant, repressing the feeling of womanhood recognition, with the permanent desire to be protected by a father. I asked for the group's feedback to encourage the practise of the adult behaviour for client X.Z. In order to eliminate the risk of any confusion and to totally avoid the child-like behaviour, I reminded them of the importance of expressing the states of the ego under the supervision of the adult Ego state.

From the perspective of the Transactional Analysis, the client has not benefited from a healthy symbiosis, and that is why she attempted to reproduce the primary pattern of transactions from her entourage. More precisely, when she was a child she did not have a mother practising with her the states of the Parent and Adult Ego, the natural states of a mother with her child; when she was brought into the family and grew up she perceived the symbiosis of an imaginary dependence of her natural mother on her grandmother, symbiosis full of contamination: her grandmother's state of Parent and Adult in symbiosis with the Child state of her mother, with the exclusion of the Adult and Parent states of the biological mother. In other words, "mother knew nothing, grandmother knew everything". The client's mother has never had a relation of real autonomy; even when she got married to her present husband she did not have the courage to tell grandmother she was leaving —she asked her daughter's help to talk to Mamma Nuța. The client's mother was devalued by her own mother (the client's grandmother) and interiorised this devaluing, which did not correct the behaviour of the client's mother; on the contrary, it brutally modified it with the perturbation of the Child state and annulment of the Parent and Adult states. Consequently, the client's mother did not succeed in being a "mother" in the true sense of the word; she was a child when she had to be an adult or a parent and failed being an adult or parent because the respective states were annulled, and the devaluing was also transmitted by Mamma Nuța by the beatings inflicted to the client or her daughter, when they were both drunk. Client X.Z. continued her devaluing in the relation with her first husband as well, whom she overvalued, and continued thus her mother's symbiosis with Mamma Nuța in the relation with her first husband, who, in order to prepare her for the world of music, used to "educate" her by salary cuts if she did not smile when supposed to, if she improvised lyrics, etc. By everything I applied in the line of therapeutic techniques, I aimed at the very correction of symbiosis, bringing to the front level the Adult and Parent states.

I considered the somatisation, more precisely the apparition of the red stains on the chest and neck, as symbols of a *"strong vascularisation, there is blood flowing under her skin"*: the client's femininity was long-time dimmed, hidden, "she must not provoke men". The woman in front of me is a very attractive woman, with true top model measurements. In fact, after the group therapeutic session, at her following appearance on the stage, when she sang, she was extremely attractive, nicely dressed, with great hair, extremely feminine. Her chest and neck are erogenous areas for the client: the somatisation zone was not random!

The session ended with my request to receive from X.Z. some drawings or paintings she considers important and we obviously set a date for receiving the materials.

On the set date I received a drawing considered significant by the client, together with some notes, thoughts, and poems written between 1993 and 1999. Furthermore, before the following group session, I had another session with client X.Z., which lasted for 4 hours, and during that session I found out the story of Mamma Nuţa and the client's questions without answer related to her birth. In the past, at the suggestion of her former husband now deceased, to find out who her biological father was, she did everything to make her mother or grandmother reveal this secret: she stopped visiting them for months or wrote letters to them at the same time; she sent them "questionnaire" letters, so all they had to do was to tick the correct answer, for instance: "*my father is: a) A; b) R;*", etc.

I shall proceed by analysing the gestalt cycle during the session. Thus, the interruption of the contact with herself and the therapist was done the moment I asked her, "what age have you reached now?". The stages of a dysfunctional behaviour succeeded then during the session (see Chapter 2):

- desentivisation – by which the client "annuls" the sensations of the supported mechanism. The client let out nothing of the sensations she was experiencing, other than those which could be noticed by her exterior. The dialogue with herself was done by writing poetry and entries in the diaries. She had come to the group with the desire to solve some problems, but there was also the risk of quarrelling with the "foreman, the team head", as it happened in the dream. In her childhood she introjected various inappropriate emotional messages: "you must not cry because you are X's grand-daughter", "you must not act in theatre plays or paint, these are not true professions", etc.

The only modalities to express emotions remained for her writing poems, writing in diaries and singing. In the therapist's practice I think desentivisation was done by practising certain behaviours meant to mask her real feelings, even show-off behaviours: rising from the chair, searching for crayons, the message being, "I want you to see me, but I am also hiding from you";

- introjection – meant to internalise the messages from parents, authorities, etc. An example of a message introjected by the client was received from her very aggressor: "if a woman refuses a man sexually, that man may die". The introjected message found its manifestation, for instance, in the client's sexual behaviour, as an adult woman (*"a woman may be responsible for a man's death during sex, if she refuses him ... that is why I cannot afford the satisfaction of orgasm, and thus I myself am sexually frustrated and then I punish my partner, and before my and his reaching orgasm I tell him I want to smoke a cigarette; we then can come back and continue the sexual intercourse"*).

- retroflection – it was apparent in the body posture of the client, the position she adopted when I initiated our dialogue: she raised her legs, crouched on the chair, embraced her knees, took off her glasses and started to rock slowly on the chair. The position described is that of a little girl, a child who is defending herself against the world, the aggressions against her, but also needing affection, needing to feel protected. The client knew and waited for me to "start" working "hypnotically" with her, permanently manifesting an expectation for "hypnosis". This hypothesis of mine as therapist, that she was waiting for "hypnosis", was confirmed also after several weeks of activity with another group (the client continued to participate in another therapy group), when she mentioned that when I looked at her she had the impression of quickly going into a trance. The emotions retained within the client's body took the somatisation form too, i.e. reddening of neck and chest, in different situations.

- deflection – by which the client interrupts the contact with the

91

therapist, as I mentioned before. The contact with me, the therapist, was cut during the session the moment she started to recount the tragedy, the church episode. The content of the account had a huge emotional load; it was brought to the surface with much pain, but I reconnected her with me by means of conversational hypnotic induction, the focus on the breath rhythm, muscular relaxation. I cautiously continued the corporal reconnection with my person. I mentioned before what the body contact with an abused client means. I think that the scene lived with the client at that time was the moment when her reconnection with herself and the world began.

- projection – by which the client projects the criticism towards the therapist and protects herself against contact. The client also had such behaviours, but under the form of "evasion", of play, like a child playing "hide and seek" (rising from the chair, drawing with crayons, answers eluding the subject approached, etc). These behaviours may be understood also as challenges for me as therapist: "is she going to be mad if I do that?". I remember that, at the first session, she asked for my permission to enact different behaviours. I was like a Parent, but she was testing me to see what kind of a Parent I was, Normative or Caring? My behaviours and answers from the Adult State surprised the client used to answers from the Parent State. Her relation with the world meant to me a co-creation of the therapeutic relationship from Adult to Adult or a functional I-You relationship.

During our discussions, I asked her about the way in which she relates to her grandmother at present. Her grandmother, Mamma Nuța, is now a very religious woman; she considers that the grandmother's close relation with the church is the consequence of the "burden she is carrying". Grandfather died many years ago; she was on tour then, but found out from relatives that whenever the door opened grandfather would ask, "Is it X.Z.?". Even today, the client is convinced that her grandfather wanted to tell her something. At the funeral, when she came home from the tour, she did not recognise her mother; she was extremely changed. At present, the two women drink less than before.

92

The client solved this problem too, in a discussion with both of them. Grandmother drinks only on Sundays before lunch, when the whole family gathers. Her mother drinks wine; she has never quit drinking entirely, and she gets easily intoxicated.

When the client read the material, she considered it opportune to complete it with some thoughts.

"11.12.2010
I met Loredana (my therapist) at 12.00 a.m. Today. I talked for about 4 hours in a row ... my brain was boiling from so many variants of the answer to one single question ... Who am I? I liked travelling back in time, with Loredana as my guide, because I succeeded in getting somehow detached (although I still get lost among the trees and fail to see the forest ... but that's why I have Lore by my side, to draw my attention when I seem to derail ...) and I keep in mind, constantly and consciously, the fact that this is the last time I remake this road. Or perhaps the first?

In the morning, still on 12.12.2010   08.05 a.m.
I will meet one of my ex-colleagues from the band today. He came to the country to sort some business. He has the same given name as my grandfather. And as I was sitting, a cup of coffee in one hand and the cigarette in the other ... I remembered how grandfather attempted to stab grandmother twice ... in the kitchen ...
I intervened each time. I yelled at them to come back to their senses ... and then I started to shake uncontrolled and to cry ... grandmother was telling me don't cry, nothing happened!!! Nothing! WTF?!? I was thinking that I was sure to blame ... they were sleeping separately since I was born, so ...
It was my fault their conflict had reached that point ... the two incidents took place one week apart ... the scenario was identical ... I did not understand why I was trembling like that, why I felt like crying, why I felt their conflict as being mine, or, more seriously, generated by me ... perhaps I was transmitted that, directly, indirectly ... it was all the same ... inside me.

After grandfather died, I started to travel to the other world and I had many conversations with him; he used to warn me if something bad was about to happen, would advise me how to avoid conflicts ... and in 2003, when I went into a coma (for a short time, during surgery, in Timişoara), it was him who sent me back, telling me that my mission was not over yet ...

... When I separated from my first husband, I wrote a poem describing our marriage; after I read the poem to him he started to cry ... it was the first time I saw him crying ... I understood that only when he was losing he could see what he had had, I told him that although it was not indifferent to me what was happening to him, I could not support him any more, and I advised him to go see a psychologist, to overcome this period. He did not do it; he kept telling me that I should remain beside him, he could not open before anyone else ... I asked him why he hadn't done it in our years together? If this is indeed what he was feeling ... he gave me no answer, he only told me I was the meanest woman, because I was not doing what he asked me to, that I did not understand his pain, or, even worse, that I was indifferent to what was happening to him ... I was not, I was hurting too because honestly I did not know how I could go on, because I felt as though I was twice as old as I actually was, I could not sing, because the only songs whose lyrics I fully remembered were Smooth Operator and I Will Survive, the rest was all blank ... so I left everything to him, all we had acquired together, and I started from zero. I saw a psychologist, I went to see a priest, because I needed to know I had made the right decision, that my mind was not wandering, as he had repeated to me so often during our marriage ... several months later, I received a phone call and found out he had died in a car crash, the car I had given to him ... the artist colleagues and his family made a statement to the newspaper accusing me of causing the accident ... I announced to everyone what happened, ironic, isn't it? And the media people said I could not be contacted ... I keep my phone opened all the time, I have the same numbers ... I would ask the person who wrote the article, quoted by the television stations, how much does it take to destroy a person?

94

And then, how can he sleep at night, having that on his conscience? OK, here's the poem [*in English in original, without corrections*]:

The dance

I asked you to dance ... you ... tired, said yes
at the smiling ladies took a final glance
and we started slowly, spinning round and round
we joined the circus, with a sceptic crowd ...
I could hear the voices, telling you to stop
sitting at the table, waiting for me to run
in the middle of the night, just like in the fairytale
but their waiting failed ...
and here we are still spinning
slightly slowin' down ...
you're too busy counting steps
and I'm nowhere to be found
I've lost myself again ... I'm no longer me
I'm just the shadow ... of what is left of me
You're so hard tryin' to guess my next faze
don't you see?!? I choke in your embrace!?!
but wait ... the lady's watchin' ...
as you step on my foot
all she does is laugh and screams:
it's all her fault!
I guess the lady's winning ...
you're the best stranger I have ever loved
we were strangers in the night
alone, but so together, now, the song has ended ... can you say
FOREVER ? [*end of fragment in English on original, without corrections*]

P.S. My former husband's mother, perfect actress, could not find the strength to take part in the funeral of her beloved son ... but she found the time and strength to make sure I would not let her without the house, amazed at finding that even after the articles and TV shows I donated the apartment to her ... of course there was one further question ... who was going to pay the bills?"

Phenomenology and field theory

The phenomenological approach means remaining as close as possible to the client's experience, staying here and now, rather than interpreting his or her behaviour; it means helping the client become aware of how he or she understood and understands the world. By the phenomenological method the client is approached with an open mind, with real curiosity: nothing is more important than discovering the client's personal experience. Within the therapeutic framework, the phenomenological method has become an investigation of the client's significance and subjective experience in the world. The method has three components (P. Joyce & C. Sills, 2001, pp. 34-46):

1- Putting between parentheses – for the therapist to be open and present in the therapeutic relations, he leaves "behind" his load of prejudices, judgements, attitudes that may influence the therapeutic relations. Nevertheless, therapists are human beings too; they can operate only sequentially, as mentioned before. Putting between parentheses does mean becoming free of prejudices, attitudes or perceptions, but remaining close to the novelty of the here-and-now moment and avoiding the danger of making hasty or premature judgements from the unique experience of the client with whom the therapeutic process is done. The recommendation to the therapists is to begin by a willing attitude of considering attitudes, options or judgements as doubtful, and that it is necessary to let some time pass before reaching any conclusion;

2- Description – supposes being aware of what is immediately obvious and describing what one sees; the therapist, after putting between parentheses hypotheses and values, will only describe what he or she observes, feels and hears, what he or she perceives from the client's acts, without interpreting it. The therapist will also observe the personal phenomenology, what he or she feels, the body strains or even the loss of interest;

3- Horizontalism or equalisation – what is in the background, unseen or absent may be important for the therapist, it may provide him with a signification about the client's behaviour.

Active curiosity means that the therapist is interested in the way the situations occur, what significance the client gives them, how things fit together, how they appear in a larger picture. When the therapist asks questions, these questions should resemble a phenomenological interrogation and not a police questioning: it is recommended to avoid asking "why?", because such a question calls for rationalisation or criticism. The questions are more efficient if we use open questions and they are focused on the client's process rather than on content. A sequence-by-sequence investigation is useful for the therapist to find out and help the client understand certain important processes which may have occurred too fast to be recognised by the client.

The field theory brings two meanings into the clinical domain debate:

a- experiential field – as awareness field of a person, a metaphor for the manner in which a client organises his or her personal experience. This field is the phenomenological field and is unique for each person;
b- extended or effective field – it includes the objective world, but also what is not within the immediate awareness range of the person, together with all the latent possibilities and potentialities of the client's self-expression.
The client actively organises the field, in accordance with his current needs, his older or newer previous field configurations, fixed gestalts or "unfinished business from the past", as they are called in the gestalt. The therapist's task is to understand how the client proceeds, what he understands, what patterns he uses in contact, what lies beyond his awareness in the extended field of possibilities and influences (op. cit., p. 47).
The most important name in the phenomenological analysis is Edmund Husserl. In his time, Europe was dominated by a Christian vision and was traversing a transition phase, from the world dominated by tradition to the modern industrial world; philosophers were those who offered

answers to people's questions, to prejudices before religious beliefs. Husserl was inspired by Descartes's thinking, but did not entirely accept the idea that man may be fulfilled only through reason and logic: he considered that an analysis of daily experience is necessary to reach the true significance of emotions, actions and relations. Phenomenology requires anisolation from the world, the existing theories and beliefs. Contemporary qualitative researchers adopt a constructivist position, i.e. the contextualised discoveries comprise one truth and not the supreme truth, unlike Husserl's opinion.

Husserl was not convinced that the phenomenological method may be used in subjects such as psychology or sociology. His purpose was to better understand human fundaments such as time, intent, colour, number. This comprehension was done by applying certain phenomenological methods on himself, on his own experience; but for this very reason one may not claim that phenomenology can be applied to other domains as well. Most therapists recommend their clients to isolate themselves from problems, to describe experiences in detail, to express experiences in a new language, to renew experiences, to understand the self and their experiences. However, from many other viewpoints therapy is not a phenomenological approach, the purpose is to highlight the existential data of the problem and of the solution to discover the essence of the matter. The therapist teaches the client how to apply the phenomenological principles described by Husserl. The phenomenological principles have opened the way for three great directions:

A)   Duquesne's school of empirical phenomenology
It attempted to code and systematise the phenomenological method in order to teach it to students, to apply it in research centres and to publish research articles. Several researchers, such as Werrz (1984), Hycner (1985), Moustakos (1994), elaborated a set of rules followed by the researchers in phenomenology:

Step 1 - collect written or verbal protocols describing the subject's experience;

Step 2 - read carefully to understand the whole;
Step 3 - extract important paragraphs;
Step 4 - eliminate irrelevant repetitions, statements that are not important for the phenomenon under study;
Step 5 - integrate these significations in one single exhaustive description of the phenomenon.

In this process the research should:

- develop an open attitude in relation with the phenomenon;

- eliminate suppositions;

- adhere to the principle of horizontality, no significance is more important than another;

- imagine what should change so that the phenomenon becomes different, what the limits of the phenomena are in order to tell the essential features from the unessential features of the phenomenon;

- develop an empathic presence towards the phenomenon described. The researcher uses description to get involved in the situation as it was experienced by the subject;

- exhibit patience in the study of the topic, in the description of the situation;

- amplify, be attentive to any detail that may be taken into consideration;

- turn from objects to imminent significations. A connection is created with the objective significations as experienced by the subject (Vertz, 1984).

B) Method of conceptual meeting
This method is an approach of phenomenological research forwarded

by Joseph De Rivera and is built on the perspective of the "human science" of the Duquesne group, with influences from the work of the German psychologist Kurt Lewin. The purpose of approach is to produce a map of personal experiences. At the core of the method lies the meeting between the investigator and the person (or client), after the latter has agreed to become a research partner. The investigator decides to study some aspects of human experience and collects personal preliminary reflections on the topic and data from the literature. The result of the study and reflection is sensitisation towards the subject and control of the ideas that may result from this phenomenon. The investigator asks questions to assist the partners in his or her presentation of different aspects of experience; after this stage, the investigator shares with the partner the ideas regarding the nature of phenomena, checks if the ideas have been understood and asks the partner if the account is in accordance with the previously described experience. By this dialogue, the investigation receives the confirmation of some features of the model and discovers if these traits are contradicted or not, requiring a revision or even a differentiation. Performing this procedure with a series of partners helps the investigator reach a final form of the essential features of the phenomenon under study. De Rivera has realised studies on emotions such as: anger, love, shame, guilt and distancing (1981).

The conceptual meeting is consequently a dialectic process in which the researcher can not only rely on his or her personal experiences or data received from informers, but also create a dynamic interaction between the two processes. The investigator is active, and verifies each part of the description.

B)   Existential-phenomenological research

The existential-phenomenological research expresses the connection between phenomenology and existentialism. Existentialism constitutes a philosophical perspective meant to understand the experience to exist in the world. Psychotherapists and existentialist philosophers use phenomenology as a method to explore the significations of existential concepts. The existential-phenomenological concept came from the renowned studies of the Scottish psychiatrist R. D. Laing, performed in the period 1958-1963. Laing chose to study schizophrenia as this disease created high responsibility in the family life of the person suffering from it. Schizophrenia is also related with the state institutions because it is a commercial help for medicine companies. The purpose of the study was to get as close as possible to the patient by using Husserl's precepts, to return to the "thing *in se*". The method was to explore the significations of the words uttered by the persons involved, of the patient, of all those involved in the co-construction of the schizophrenia phenomenon: patients, family members, therapists. The researcher describes the experience in two different manners, first by narrating it, and second in a pragmatic manner. The narrative construction uses words of the patients and family members without exaggerating with interpretation. The second is the result of a series of existential concepts, i.e. ontological insecurity, incorporation, falseness, collision, etc. The result of the research is the natural attitude of comprehending the phenomenon, as in that period when society saw illness as "natural", caused by genes or "biology". The author's research led to a new vision on schizophrenia, i.e. what was meaningless before became metaphoric, and described the relation and the state of being. The study used the concept of "demystification" to describe what was attempted. The group of authors examined the situations when daily experiences operated not only to cover the true nature of what was happening, back to the "thing *in se*", but also to help the groups of psychiatrists and specialists. They practised a critical phenomenology to contradict the moral bases of certain actions. In fact, they used the phenomenological approach to enhance or change the description of the phenomenon, and then a re-description or a new modality to see things, precisely to support interpretation. The stages mentioned before cannot operate in the absence of a phenomenological analysis. Consequently, the effect of research depends on the combination of phenomenological strategies with the hermeneutic ones.

Phenomenology is one of the basic methods of qualitative research; most researches use the procedures highlighted by Husserl:

- Framing suppositions;
- Expanding horizons;
- Exhaustive description;
- Discovery of the phenomenon essence.

Although phenomenology has a central position in social sciences, there are a series of limitations associated to the way in which phenomenology research is applied in psychotherapy. Not anyone can perform a phenomenological survey, even if they use the recommendations from guides by the book, as philosophic arguments are also necessary. Three factors influence the phenomenological research and limit somehow the performance of studies:

- Marginalisation of phenomenological research by psychology and social sciences;
- Husserl's stress on the "ecological", on the personal style and researcher, determines the choice of some topics that are very easily demonstrated;
- Most studies are presented in journals with limited distribution and the public has difficulty in analysing and criticising them.

The new phenomenology associated with researchers Van Kaam, Georgi and Duquesne represents a distortion of Husserl's ideas. Thus, phenomenology becomes subjective and explores people's experiences in a subjective manner; whereas the old phenomenology studies the objects of human experience.

The fusion between phenomenology and hermeneutics lies at the basis of Husserl's activity and probably the most important quality of his research comes form the fact that both traditions are necessary to study the dynamics of daily life. The qualitative research refers to finding a balance between phenomenology and hermeneutics;

nevertheless, in psychotherapy there is no clear comprehension yet of the epistemologies presented: phenomenology is reduced to the description of personal experiences, and hermeneutics to an interpretation.

Consequently, the phenomenology initiated by Husserl aimed at stabilising the fundament of knowledge, at building a sure basis, starting from the manner in which objects and phenomena are perceived by the conscious and continuing with the way the preconscious and unconscious include them. The 19th century studies stressed the role of primary sensorial-perceptive experiences. The 4wesgestult therapy was exclusively based on laboratory, meant only to introduce the idea of psychic phenomenon and behaviour into the physical reality. On the clinical side of this development psychoanalysis appeared, based also on a psychological knowledge, but by means of building another type of knowledge. The qualitative research also stresses knowledge, being a legitimate form of science applied to human beings and relationships. The phenomenological psychological research aims at clarifying the situations lived by persons in every-day life, but also at remaining faithful to the phenomenon and context in which it occurs; the purpose is to capture as closely and correctly as possible the manner in which the phenomenon is experienced within a context. Thus, phenomenology searches for the psychological signification lying at the basis of the phenomenon by investigating and analysing certain experiences lived in the participants' life (Jonathan A. Smith, co-ord, 2008). In order to test the method one uses the phenomenon of learning as research means, as the participants describe the situation easily, without being inhibited in any way. However, in order to obtain as many perspectives as possible on learning, one may collect descriptions, examples of the failure to learn, as well. The term is used to describe the phenomenological method. If a better comprehension is intended, for instance, one will study the way in which learning was done in daily life, in the "living world", as it is called in phenomenology. Phenomena may be learned in every-day life, in varied environments, and they may be learned or not. In the phenomenological study, both situations are presented from the viewpoint of the experience of the participants in the survey. The participants, after a general introduction on the purpose of research, are asked to describe a situation when they failed in the learning process. The abstract of descriptions for two participants is described in the paper of Giorgi (1985) from the work of J. A. Smith (2008, p. 30).

So that I as therapist can place myself as close as possible to the client's field, to grasp the manner in which the client structured her experience along time, what cycles she used, I considered it important for the co-creation of the therapeutic relation to analyse some materials received from the client. I have already mentioned that I do not do that with all clients, but each client may be put to value by expressing the therapist's interest for some of the products of his or her activity. For me as therapist it is very important to have landmarks in the practice activity, in my labour with the client. By reading some fragments, poems, by the analysis of some materials received from the client with his or her agreement, I may foresee my intervention action; I perceive which objective must be fulfilled or negotiated with the client. I consider that the analysis of the material received is similar to a phenomenology analysis. I further on present fragments from the materials received from client X.Z., when she was 16 and 17. They are fragments of her diaries, materials received between the group sessions. At home, the client reread the diaries corresponding to the "age reached after each group session". I admired the client's motivation to put an end to her suffering and the trust she granted me as therapist. The therapeutic relation was co-created with each group session, every time when she brought me further fragments from her diaries. She was patiently waiting for the end of the group session and for reaching the final report and especially eager to "complete" it. It is obvious that such clients with artistic inclinations and with the willingness to "write" their return to the world are not an every-day occurrence, but the therapist identifies the modalities of engaging the client in his or her own reconstruction.

"*12 May 1993 – 11.45 p.m.*

I started to tell ... the diary what happened in childhood ... I accounted the beginning ... I am scared and I don't know why, I feel like crying. I AM AFRAID!!

Lory, why aren't you near me? What will Cristi think of me after he reads what I have written here? [Lory was a friend of that period]

Will he understand me? I hope so ... I don't know if he will believe me, but it is all true, and it is only a part ... If he knew how bad I am sometimes! Corina, pray for me, pleaseIt is night and I am home alone Oh, my God!

Help me!
Please!"

"*13 May 1993*

Dear diary ... nothing, nothing, nothing, ...

I talked to Corina today, she told me that she also thought of me, at the same time, late at night ... I was glad to hear that ... maybe God listened to me too, for once ... if I did not believe in Him, I might have committed suicide at 12 or 13, when my grandmother had her drinking problem out of control ... she kept scolding me, day after day, I cried night after night, I wanted to run away from home or to take something, to be taken to E.R. ... or to die ... to reach God. But now she has changed, I love her, although she does not understand me, she loves me ... and this is enough for me ..."

"*14 May 1993* [in English in original without corrections]*I don't trust myself, why?*

I feel so bad, so crazy, so mad!

I will call myself Maddy, from MAD.

I'm nervous" [end of the fragment in English in original without corrections]

"*23 June 1993*

School holiday at last ...

I want to become a writer and a poet!

You, my diary, what do you think? I started to write the second novel, Fatal obsessions.

105

I was invited to go to Doman, but I would have to stay at G.I. and I don't like it, in fact I don't know why I worry so much, what is done is done ... what the hell ... I am no longer 8 years old, I am 16.
Maddy"

"*5 January 1994*
in the evening, I think, 5 January ...
CATASTROPHE! APOCALYPSE HAS COME!
Mother told me that if I got bad marks in the second trimester, she wouldn't let me take canto lessons any more!"

"*8 January 1994*
I came back from Doman several hours ago ... I sang to him Ioane, Ioane ... [a Romanian song] *(Ha, ha, ha everybody is asleep, but I cannot sleep).*
How easy it is to arrive from dreams to nightmares ... I can no more ... I am tired of speaking so much about myself."

"*13 January 1994*
PEOPLE SHOULD NOT BE JUDGED, BUT UNDERSTOOD!
I don't like being alone, solitude makes me be lost in dreams, in the past, in the future, memories, hopes ...
I hope that soon I will find out who I really am.
I really hope so.
I hope so and I am praying for it."

"*18 January 1994*
9 p.m.
"I feel as though I had betrayed myself. I thought it was all over, but it is not ...
ALL I WANT IS EITHER AN END OR A BEGINNING. WHICH OF THEM REALLY DESERVES WAITING FOR? THE BEGINNING OR THE END? Do I really wish the end?
I am very very very nervous.
10.20 p.m.

I am crying and I don't know why ... I feel so lonely, I can't wait leaving this house ... being alone, I hate myself, I HATE MYSELF! Or I wish to change, but how, where, when ... I feel so weak, so abandoned ...
MOTHER!
OH! LORD!
I want to know who I am
I want to know WHAT MY PURPOSE IS
I want to be alone ...
I am alone, I am sad
I am abandoned and my heart is barren
                    Good night!"

"7 March 1994
I deserve nothing, I deserve nothing, I deserve not even to live ... Oh God, how I wish to be alone some place, where I could do what I want. I am sick again, I feel that history is repeating with me. It does not go forward, but keeps repeating itself. I wish to give the diary to my mother ... I am so afraid, will she understand me? ... maybe. I feel like crying ... I was so joyous yesterday ... today however ..."

Session no. 7

The session started, although two participants were absent, calling in sick. The session started with the request for insights from all participants during the week since our previous session. Client X.Z. mentioned she felt very well, she appreciated: "*I reached the age of 21. I sang very relaxed in the club and I dressed my hair in Marilyn Monroe style; many people asked if the singer had changed ... I sang without glasses, the club was full of men, I felt very well ...*". As the client was speaking in a relaxed manner, I asked for her permission to approach the issues of sexuality, "to clean up" if there was something there. The client agreed and I understood that if she had libido, in the moments of maximum intensity, she used to tell the partner, "*let's stop for a while and smoke a cigarette, and continue afterwards*". I returned to her age of 12 and her fears of becoming a

107

woman, when she was with the family of grandfather's "friends". She realised that since then she has been horrified of being kissed on the mouth, of being touched, and if this happened, she would immediately shudder. Sex was associated with death: "if a woman refuses a man, he dies; it is women who provoke men". Consequently, all men must die, obviously in a symbolic form … In her sexual life she is domineering, *"like a sort of revenge against men and, as punishment, I refuse the final pleasure. I understand it now, I used to tell the partner to go smoke a cigarette"*. Under the pretext of the Christmas fasting, she stopped having sex with her husband. Her attitude when she confessed it was ambivalent, and in order to cox her into making a decision, I asked her if she was still breathing in the fasting period, or if she was still eating … we know we have some fundamental needs inherited from Maslow … The client started to laugh. My further intervention for the client and the participants was to stress and accept their womanhood. The client confessed she has reread the diaries between the ages of 10 and 20 and has analysed the events described from the perspective of the Transactional Analysis of the ego's states. The discussion turned towards the relationships between men and women in the couple; one of the participants concluded that each person in the relationship is Adult, Child, Parent, as he or she chooses to be, to produce joy to the other. I encouraged client X.Z. to adopt the Adult Ego state and to take over not only her own sexuality: the symbolic punishments are no longer necessary and obviously her husband is prepared for her. Impatiently and with a sharp sense of humour, the client could not wait to get home! The discussion continued with a short presentation of the concept of "castrating woman"; the inner dialogue continued also after I finished talking, surely, for each woman in the group …

The clients were ready for interventions of ego strengthening and I applied the metaphor of my personal counsellor. The induction of trance was without problems; the intervention went as follows:

"You imagine yourself in an environment filling you with warmth, peace and quiet, the feeling of comfort and respect for yourself. You

may search in your memories to find that place or you can create it yourself. And focus your attention upon the details of this place to be able to experience them with all senses, to have a poignant feeling of being there. When looking around, some place near, you will see a path going into the horizon. You take this path, wandering at will, at your pace, until suddenly you will glance in the distance a white-bluish shine, slowly coming towards you without being scary at all. And as it is drawing nearer and nearer, you realise that in reality it is a living being: maybe a person you know, perhaps a friendly animal. And please observe this being as well as you can to grasp all the details about it. Try to determine its gender, to see the traits of the face, the hair, the build. Try to see it as clearly as possible; if this being generates feelings of warmth, peace and quiet and safety, it is obvious you have met your personal counsellor (the ideomotor response is required when the personal counsellor occurs).

And being aware of this, ask your counsellor his or her name, and then ask him or her to help you solve the problem you are facing. Start a conversation with your counsellor, talk to him about the problems and troubles, as if you were talking to a very close friend, and ask your personal counsellor the questions about you for which you wish to find an answer. And focus all your attention on the answers he gives you that can be formulated verbally during the entire discussion or under the form of symbolic gestures. For instance: by showing you an object or bringing it before your eyes, knowing that although for the moment you have not understood all he has told you, you will be able to think afterwards and find the meaning, the profound sense of the things communicated".

Time is taken and confirmation is required by ideomotor response ...

"And when you have your answers to your present questions, thank your counsellor for his answers and make arrangements with him how you can connect again to talk some more, to search for answers to your questions again and again; and when you have an agreement to meet again, bid you counsellor farewell and get ready to return home".

Each participant described the images and sensations experienced during the metaphor. The relaxation occurred rapidly, and the images experiences were flashes combining part of the representations of each, but also related to the daily activities. What was interesting for each client was the state of calmness and inner peace they experienced. Client X.Z. identified her favourite place in Peru, where she was "*great priestess, and the guide as an intensely golden light. I received the expected answer and I saw my husband holding me*".

The session ended by suggesting as homework for each participant to think about her own sexuality.

When she read the material I had written, the client added the following:

"*2011, the year of the winner ...*
the year when I shall show to those who are ready to see how in a crisis year ... you can make a profit ... the spring when those who want to understand will understand how, from the crisis of identity, one may come out as a Winner! Ana-Maria, today is your "birthday", each day is your day, since the first day ... this will be my projection for the year to come
to my husband, with whom, according to the scenario, I started a conflict [rhyme poetry in original in Romanian – translator's note]

> *you, with the sexual gland, I, with the pineal gland*
> *and, from my astral world ... I underline your mistake*
> *Do you want to see? You Do Not Want To See!!*
> *Do you want to feel? Do you only want to feel? ... well, why do you lie to yourself?*
> *You look at me, ..., do you see her?!? why are you punishing me like this?*
> *It is not I who abandoned you, it is not I who ran away*
> *To the "good relatives" ... damn your family!*
> *Why do you want me to care? It is your life lesson,*
> *So set your mind (and heart) and learn*
> *Wake up, assume your responsibility*

*When you turn the knife in the wound ... even so, are you not
afraid?!?*
*Not of me ... of that mother of yours ... that she takes you and
runs away*
And she gets lost from you again ... and leaves you abandoned,
To clean her mess. What a dog life she gives you!
And you still side with her ... and hide, behind my back ...
When she rejects you, you don't understand that she complains
And expects from you ... all you can take from me ...
*But I do not want to give her anything ... nor do I wish to take
you*
You are always her Son,
For now, ..., my husband
*Tell me now, what do you choose? To love without
understanding?*
It is mere pseudo-love ... drowned in unawareness
You say, I don't want to know about mothers and children
But then, why do you weep when your heart's in turmoil
*Tells you that She lies to you ... she does not have a clue what
she feels ...*
*That she is only a bitch, not the "mother", she barks and bites,
out of fear*
*She feeds you, ..., when she wants to and beats you, just like
that!*
She rejects and attracts you, she plays and draws back ...
*You, Now, are my husband! Her Son ... you will always be her
son*
Stop betraying me ... with Her ...
I am a Woman ... not a bitch".

The materials received are an endless source of interpretation of the
client's conscious and unconscious content. The husband has a
"sure" mother, whereas the client has always asked herself who her
mother might be. The feeling of belonging and property were sources
of analysis for the client: to whom does she belong? What is the
client sure to have? (It is difficult for a person to constantly ask

himself or herself who the father is and sometimes actually who the mother is.) The projection was done on the person closest to her, her husband. Surely one will apply some techniques of the client's ego strengthening. Gradually, and at her own pace, the client was remaking the contact with herself and with the world, with partial evaluations on my part for the behavioural, emotional, cognitive and biologic levels. I was encouraging any change having occurred in the four behavioural domains and I was focused on the maintaining of the therapeutic relation if possible on the level of the state of the Adult ego.

Session no. 8

The session started with an "upset" client's account after a discussion with another colleague, from outside the group. Together with the client, I analysed, from the positions of the ego's state, the transactions done and the symbiosis practised by the client and her colleague, from the position of the Ego states of Parent, Rebel Child, with the annulment of the other Ego states. Whenever we were analysing the Ego states, it was a good opportunity for all clients to analyse and continue the dialogue with themselves outside the group as well. I consider that the Transactional Analysis is useful, along with other techniques for strengthening the ego. On the conscious level one analyses the Ego states, the Adult Ego state is "mastered", gently, with a sense of humour and the client is incited to play "the Adult" in real life. Thus, the reaction of one client was, *"We need to take the T.A. course too"*. After each client talked about the important events they considered worth mentioning, I asked client X.Z. what she had to say. As the winter holidays had passed and the group session took place immediately after, the client related a meeting with a group of friends, herself, her husband and another three persons, when she described in detail a threesome sex encounter (herself, a female friend and a male friend), which occurred many years ago, after her divorce and the death of her first husband. I asked permission to analyse the particular event, with focus on the following questions:

112

- Why did she tell the story in the presence of her current husband?
- Why were there two women and one man in that sexual act?
- Why did it occur after the death of her first husband?

As therapist, I connected with the accounts read in the client's diary and I was expecting many significations for the client to surface. It was a session when my intuition told me more than ever that I could not afford to losing any of the client's words:

- The client's main defence mechanism was the identification with the aggressor, coming into action on the occasion of the erotic act;
- The account of the story in the presence of her husband was an "invitation" for him to continue, at least symbolically, the action of the aggressor interiorised by the client.
- In her sexual relation with her first husband, the client did not feel a true woman: she was dominated, and her sexual initiatives ignored. As another "aggressor" disappeared, and died, i.e. her former husband, the client felt "free" to experiment, under another form of "aggression", the sexual relation with other persons, by dominating the female partner. The sexual scene allowed the reinterpretation of the client's sexual role in her first marriage; the sexual role played in the scene with the other two friends was a re-enactment of the role of aggressor from her childhood. The role played by the female friend and the male sexual partner were perceived as "insignificant"; as, in fact, the little girl, when abused, dissociated and was hoping for everything to end as soon as possible.

The account of the sex scene with certain "details" was made in the presence of her husband. When asked what made her describe the scene in his presence, she mentioned that she wished to observe his reactions. I asked myself if maybe her motivation was to provoke the current husband to be her future "aggressor" in sexual life. To verify this hypothesis, I asked the client, "what did the account arouse in your husband?" She said that some behaviour changes had occurred in their sex life. I did not formulate the interpretation. I was expecting a possible resistance from the part of the client, and then I initiated a discussion about femininity, the enigma of womanhood and especially the power a woman may have over men in general and especially on her husband. She remembered the metaphor of the white wolf and the black wolf; I told her to think about it and decide which wolf she wanted to feed.

Between the two sessions, I received the following materials from the client (*rhymed poetry, in original in Romanian*):

> "*I write, I eat,*
> *I eat and write,*
> *I digest emotions,*
> *I want to know!*
> *I neither offer, nor refuse*
> *I feel no more abuse*
> *I seek to know who I am,*
> *What my holy role is!*
> *I want love, that's what I ask for*
> *I also want what I offer*
> *I do not want only part of the whole,*
> *Not even half is enough*
> *From ecstasy to agony*
> *There is not more than an eternity*
> *I traverse it and I don't even know ...*
> *I am outside, it is deserted*
> *All I want is to be ...*" (12.12.2010)

After having read the materials, the client added a text written in English. When I suggested the client make a decision about which wolf to feed in the future: she sat next to me – below the level of my armchair – and told me she would decide which wolf to feed; she started saying in English that she would be a winner. I underlined her strength once again and what beautiful things she would be able to accomplish in the future. It was rather difficult for the client to decide what language to speak, but I considered that for her English was the language behind which she could hide: it is the language in which she sings, the language of the sub-personality she showed to the world, it is Andrada's language (Andrada is her stage-name). It is interesting how she reunited the two sub-personalities, when she wrote a material in "Andrada's language" in which she spoke about Ana-maria (*in English in original, without corrections*):

"Natural born sinner (singer)
my name is Ana-maria and I am a natural born sinner searchin' for salvation. Just like you. Society told me I am the result of an abortion. My family told me I'm the result of a sin. My mother told me I'm a child of love.

Growin' up in a communist country, with such tags, it's not easy. My birth certificate is dated 2 weeks later ... they thought I will die ... the doctors said I aint got a chance to live. They said I wont talk, I wont walk, that I might be retarded ... due to my premature coming into this world. Your world! Our world! Gods creation. I was given my mother's maiden name ... as a child, and my towns favourite gossip topic during my childhood, was a game called: "who's the father?" I started askin' myself, who is my father? I didn't get any answer ... I only got a wall of silence in which I've hurt myself every time I tried to break it down. The wall grew thicker and taller. I could hardly see the light, above me, I could barely hear the voices around me ... it was also offerin' me protection, so I helped buildin it ... by creatin' my own world, behind this wall. The wall of wonders, of questions, of doubts, of uncertainties, hate, rejection, deceptions ... all the shit that people can have inside.

I thought that I dont need to break down the wall, but it started changin' shape ... it became a prison. Was I guilty, to be imprisoned? Of what?

The silence told me that I might be guilty ... my mom's silence told me that I'm guilty ... I couldnt realize that she was weak ... ... I could feel that, but I could never see it clearly ... I was just a child, alone, against the world.

In order to find the acceptance I needed, from my "heavenly" father I denied my mother. I blamed her for not being able to tell the free-setting truth.

I accused her for not being a real mother, if she can't feel the pain she causes me by hiding behind lies. I begged her, to set herself free and to give me the peace of mind I needed to go my own way. She cried, and in return to my sufferin, my pleadin on my knees, bleeding inside my soul ... she said ... she's into too much pain ... to go back there and bring out the truth.

She couldn't find any strength left, to save her and to release me. I thought it is my incapacity of explaining how crucial this was for me, I blamed me ... for being weak, for making those around me suffer ... so, I went back to my prison, my cell ... yes the landscape changed ... the walls were different, but I was the same. I felt like a natural born sinner, yet I wanted to be forgiven ... and accepted!

Since God wasn't givin' me any signs, obvious signs, I thought I should find my own salvation, my own God, inside ... so, I started writin my own "writings on the wall", on my prison walls, in poetry ... I started praising the Lord, in my singin ... I started picturin' him, and me, as his child, in my paintings ... I started writin to him, and to me, also ... in my journals ...

I started walking his way ... the moment I stopped questioning ... the answers came. Revealed, one by one, as I was growin stronger and getting closer to my truth. The only one that really matters to me ... ... the only one that should matter to all of you ...

My name is Ana-maria. I am one of Gods beautiful creations. Just like you ...

I'm a natural born WINNER!" (end of the fragment in English in original without corrections).

For me, as therapist, when I read the material added by the client I was satisfied that my therapeutic efforts with the client had respected the zone of primal development, that I considered important, as mentioned before, to balance GIVING and RECEIVING, so that the client should not be overwhelmed. I often think that "the road to hell is paved with good intentions". In my personal development and in my own therapy I had to struggle with myself a lot to eliminate the Saviour inside me. It is very interesting how the pair dance between the therapist and the client is done in a beneficial synchronisation. I asked myself as well what need I had had to write about this case?! The motivation of describing the case was initially completely different, a paper to finish my supervision for hypnosis and Ericksonian psychotherapy, and then to publish a chapter in a work with a team of integrative psychotherapists from the European Institute of Integrative Psychotherapy, so that finally I could attach it to my model of therapeutic intervention. Somewhat, the success of X.Z. meant my success as well, but why and to what extent? I expect to find the answer to that question some time.

Session no. 9

The session was after New Year's Eve: the clients talked about where they had spent it and what they had done, and what goals they had set for the new year. I asked each participant to identify the impact of the group themes of the two previous sessions for their inner selves. Thus, they made decisions for their personal, interpersonal and professional level; each client has her own "honey jar" and, when she considers it necessary, she will take from it what she needs. Then we opened the topic of love and I suggested a game: in twos, holding hands, each should look into the colleague's eyes and search for love ... The mirrors were remarkable and for 10 minutes each took contact with herself and discovered reluctances, the courage to bear the partner's look; in fact, in real life the courage to initiate and maintain healthy interpersonal relations. After the feedback from each client, I continued by the therapeutic metaphor of "**WHITE LIGHT**"
(after Glenn Harold).

"And now ... you may wish to focus your attention ... on an area in the middle of your forehead, ... so that your entire concentration ... becomes completely focused ... on this point, ... from this area ... And now, ... you may imagine this point ... as a tiny sphere made of

117

white light ... now floating before your forehead, ... floating in the air, ... precisely over your forehead ... And this tiny sphere of light, ... is totally ... in its size and aspect, ... like a small star ... at a distance; ... a very shiny star, ... sparkling in the night sky ... radiating energy and light ... and very soon you can feel ... a sort of tickling ... or a comfortable warm shine, ... as you are becoming aware of the radiant light ... shining more and more ... as it continues to float ... before your forehead ...

And now ... you can see this tiny sphere of white light ... beginning to slowly float upwards, ... rising slightly in the air, ... higher ... and higher ... until it reaches a point ... right above your head ... and it is floating there ... above your head ... And as the sphere is beginning to grow in size ... to expand ... becoming brighter and brighter ... And you are becoming aware of its radiations ... of this shiny object ... you see the purity of its colours ... like the pure white of fresh snow ... and you feel the radiant warmth ... like the tender light in a home ... you can even hear its slight vibrations ... as it is becoming larger ... and larger ... radiating more and more shiny light ... as it is growing ... and becoming like a large ball ... And instinctively you are becoming conscious ... of its healing properties ... feeling its radiant energy ... it can heal the illness ... it can remove any discomfort ... it can revive and give energy to anything it touches ... as it is floating there ... over your head ... shining more and more powerfully, ... And you feel attracted by this healing energy ... more ... and more ... as you are feeling its purity ... and the inherent kindness ... knowing that its healing properties ... have no boundaries ... when they search ... and ... destroy ... any illness or discomfort ... And you will want to immerse ... into this radiant energy ... to bathe in its purity ... knowing you benefit from ... its wonderful healing power ... And now ... as you are thinking about this ... the sphere starts to open slowly ... flooding you with this healing energy of the white light ... energy that will give you vitality ... and will balance you, ... energy that will cleanse and cure each part of you ... And the flow of free energy ... starts flowing downwards ... And you feel this current of healing energy ... penetrating freely each part of your body ... downwards ... through

118

the top of your head ... removing any negative thoughts and emotions ... and settling new feelings of well-being ... balancing you ... as it is going down ... on your neck and shoulders ... removing any tension there ... and then along your back ... penetrating each muscle and nerve ... from the spinal cord ... removing any toxin that might be gathering there ... And as this fountain of energy ... made of pure white light ... keeps going down like a waterfall ... is flowing into each cell --- the entire body .... Cleansing you, reviving you ... healing you ... and rejuvenating you ... and you can begin to feel more and more lifted up ... more alive ... more alive than you have felt in a long while ... as health ... and well-being ... are starting to echo in your body ...

And now ... as the flow of energy ... keeps flowing through your body ... you see this energy of pure white light ... circulating freely through each organ of yours ... in the chest and stomach ... cleansing each artery and each vein ... purifying every muscle and every bone ... as it continues to glow ... down ... to the legs ... to the toes ... And now ... you can concentrate this flow of energy ... to a certain part of your body ... a part that may need more healing ... and I shall let you a while ... so that you can direct the energy ... where you need it the most, ...

[a pause of 1- 2 minutes, then I continued]

And now, ... as you keep letting this energy of white light ... go through every part of yourself ... removing any blockages ... cleansing and purifying ... each part of you ... you can imagine the white light above your head ... which has become larger and larger, ... so large ... that its healing energy ... has gone through your entire body now ... and you are completely immersed in it ... from the top of your head to the tips of your toes ... completely bathed in this source of radiant energy ... which keeps flowing freely inside and outside your body ... bringing you wonderful feelings of health and vitality ... and you know that you can view this white light full of energy any time ... penetrating your body ... and healing any part of yourself ... so that you shall continue to encourage ... the feeling of well-being and health ... in your mind ... in your body ... in your spirit ...

And now, ... the healing process is complete ... You see the mass

119

of energy over your head ... shrinking to the size of a large ball ... and the energy flow starts to diminish ... more and more ... until it stops in the end ... the white sphere above your head is closing in ... leaving you with feelings of vitality and health ... and a general feeling of well-being ... and you will notice now ... how good you are feeling ... both physically and mentally ... and emotionally ... and this wonderful healing process has reached its end ... you imagine the sphere ... still floating above your head ... slowly ... slowly ... starting to shrink ... smaller and smaller ... until it is again a little distant star ... starting to descend, ... floating slowly ... to the area before your forehead ... where it is absorbed ... back into your conscience ... and you shall become more and more conscious ... of how revived you are feeling ... as if your entire system ... your mind and body ... were purified and cleansed ... in this wonderful process of total healing ... which you can continue ... any time you wish ..."

The trance was experienced by each client with emotions, the induction was done through a naturalist trance. The hypoacusic client followed the instructions to a certain point by reading the words from my lips. It is known that the therapist reduces the tone of voice, uses more pauses, etc, and after a certain time she succeeded in self-inducing her trance, closed her eyes and her unconscious started to work; she chose a luminous valley, with many lilies in blossom (she herself bears the name of a flower) and she lived the joy and beauty of her favourite spot: "I was running to catch the sunbeams". I had never had hypoacusic clients in therapy and it was for the first time when, by lip reading, the client went into a trance. Before the exercise, I told her that, if she wants to, she may be an observer. She proved to want something else; to go into a trance too. We agreed to meet in the practice on a later date to work more intensely at the client's teaching to self-induce the hypnotic trance. Each participant sent the light where she considered necessary, to those parts of their body which required more attention. Client X.Z. realised she could transpose on different planes rather fast and she could return "here and now" equally fast. The feedback (*in English*) the client X.Z. gave to each colleague was quite interesting:

120

- the hypoacusic client - *wonder woman* - as superwoman, with formidable progress in record time;

- the client who is a registered nurse - *cat woman* - very strong, takes the adversary by surprise;

- the client who is a doctor - *woman in love* - the woman who has a lot to offer in love;

- the client who is a university teacher - *the queen* - from whom you can learn a lot, with whom you can have a conversation on any topic, with much affection,

- the client who is a teacher - *black magic woman* - with a lot of magic in her eyes, with feelings of maternal love, much closer to God;

- the therapist - *American woman* - "I am here to help you, if you want; if you don't, it is all right".
Furthermore, client X.Z. mentioned the peace and quite she felt, especially after the last session, when she learned to be more feminine. The relationship with her husband had got better, the relationship with her mother had become more authentic. The client thought of offering a surprise to her mother and inviting her to a trip to Paris, for two weeks, the desire of the client being to have a "final" discussion with her about her father's identity. During the session, when I was working with the group, I noticed that the client was writing with her left hand and in reverse, from the right to the left, in the mirror; at the end I asked her if she agreed to give me what she had written. Although it was more difficult to read, the client had written, *"my mother is maria"*, *"you are the perfect mother"*. For her, the doubts related to her natural mother had disappeared; she reconsidered her relationships with her husband and her mother, "we the two daughters of Mamma Nuţa", called Mamma Nuţa to reassure her that "your girls are doing well in Paris" (the

state of Normative Parent was thus "reassured" and the states of Adapted Child were in symbiosis). As therapist I was a little sceptical as regards the discussions in Paris. The signal was that the state of Adult ego had not supervised the state of Child ego. The client's intent in Paris was to tell her mother she loved her, and that she had found out who her father was. Several days before the group session, her mother assured her that she was born out of much love and that she would never have given her up by abortion. The client had chosen Paris because it is a city of love and of "a new beginning".

At the end of the session, I received some excerpts from the 19-year-old diary of client X.Z.

"14.12.1994

I hate myself sometimes. Why? But now I am very fond of me. I envelop myself in this love and try to create a wall enabling me to ignore the opinions of others. The problem is I don't quite succeed. It doesn't matter. I am stopping here.

... wait a minute, I am not through. I've reached the conclusion that I hate everybody who has that physical perfection I lack. I always blame it to that when I fail in something I try. God! I feel like crying! And I can do nothing to prevent it. If only there were one single problem. But there are more, oh God, if I get rid of one, others remain. This is me, mocking trouble. Will I ever be able to get rid of these complexes? Not being afraid that when I meet someone, that someone will mock me?

I hate you, world, for what you are and for what you are doing to me! You are so cruel with me, and so mean. I can beat you only in my dreams and not even then, because morning always comes and the song ends ... There, in my dreams, I am someone else. In fact, it is still I, but better, more beautiful and maybe even more intelligent ... That's that."

It is likely that the material received was not random; most complexes have been solved. The material received may also be interpreted as a challenge to the therapist so that I verify myself if I have something more to work at with the client or not. In fact, she asked me if she could join another group or not. Before I could reply, she went on, "*I shall have more than 10 sessions, unlike my colleagues!*". Only then did I reply with "as you wish" and then she stared at me and I assured her she might come. I had the feeling she was about to reiterate the complex of abandonment, but I was not "biting" her bait either. She was still playing psychological games. I let the client decide if she wanted to continue the activity with another group, where she could benefit from other interventions. The client "had grown up", but she needed further interventions to strengthen her ego, to practise some authentic behaviours and to validate them. She had got contracts in the country and she also had sent a CD to Germany with music recorded by her as a singer, and the feedback was positive. From the professional viewpoint there were no difficulties of adaptation. The colleagues in the band realised something had changed in her and wished the singer they knew back. The client mentioned she no longer asked people to call her by her stage-name; she wanted to be introduced by her given name: "I like it better". She decided to keep what she had acquired within the group, the management of sub-personalities and to stop somatisations. As the names are similar, the musical world in the town got acquainted with the change rather fast. When she read the material, the client added:

"*I want to thank Loredana for the patience to "bring me up"; the ladies in the group for their direct or indirect support ... ah, Lore, "you forgot" to tell that I called myself* [in English] *"woman of wands" to be continued ... a.m.*"

Had I actually forgotten it?! The client asked me if in the material there would remain the name X.Z. or not. I asked her what name was the most comfortable for her, and she decided for Ana-maria, her given name. So, the Ana-Maria case ...

Session no. 10

The entire group knew it was their last session and a slight trace of regret was lingering among the participants. The discussions started with the account of a painful event in the family of one colleague and the analysis of the manner in which she had intervened in her son's family. The suggestions were to act from the position of Adult. Each client underlined the changes in her behaviours, during the ten sessions, changes perceived either gradually or suddenly, but irrespective of the awareness manner, the changes were experienced with satisfaction. Client X.Z. decided to continue with a new group and we decided to go out together for a tea in the city once a month.

Whenever client X.Z. spoke, I asked for examples about her integration into family and society, examples highlighting her behavioural changes, and her accounts were topics of meditation for some participants. I mentioned that, from one session to the next, client X.Z. was rereading her diaries and had more and more explanations for her behaviours; she saw that period with different eyes, had different explanations for the behaviours of the others towards her and the attitude of her mother. In fact, during the entire period of the group session, the client reread her life story through what she had written over the years. I also received, according to our contract, some of the materials she had written, and we agreed that, after the final elaboration of my material, the client would add what she would deem necessary from her reality. It was an exchange of love, commitment and willingness to heal, to put an end to a pain that seemed endless to her. From one session to the next, the participants were more and more authentic, more powerful, with a higher desire to reintegrate into the world. The client then left for Paris and I included her in another group of personal development, for another 10 sessions.

The client's return from Paris proved to be far from her expectations. The talk with her mother never took place, so the client had not brought about the topic of her father's identity. The old patterns of interaction came back, she felt blocked before her mother's child-like behaviour, she became again the person supposed to take care of her mother (reversed role). The reality was not as she expected; at the first session with the new group, after half an hour of conversation, she however realised the progress she had made:

- No matter how hard it was, she felt the supervision of the Adult Ego state in the other states of the ego;

- The uncomfortable feeling experienced during the entire period, without triggering true scenes of "drama" with her mother, was borne, she attempted to set small goals to reach every day;

- For the first time she experienced the "withdrawal" generated by the "break" of expectations having guided her life until now, and she experienced it "live", together with her mother, who behaved as she had always behaved with her daughter;

- she accepted her mother's reality; it was Ana-maria who came out of a "dream";

- she wrote a letter to her mother, a letter she had never sent, and read it in the group. The role of the letter was of emotional catharsis and it was written in "Andrada's language", in English, and signed Maria-ana, the name being reversed (from Ana-maria) (*in English in original without corrections*)

"letter to my mom ...
(how my dream turned into my worst, awake, nightmare)
    City of light ... city of love ... so they say, at least ... but who are they? well, "they" can be anyone. Your friends, your family, your enemies ... or it can be you ... multiplied into everyone - or just you simplified in the reflection of you in everyone you meet, see ...
    God must have a hell of a plan lined up for me, since he's been giving me such big lessons. Maybe they are not even that big, or hard those lessons, maybe its just my imagination ... or paranoia.

I always felt welcome in Paris. not this time. not totally. Guess what? I had my mother with me. It was supposed to be great. two artists in a wonderful city, full of all kinds of artists ... for a few days I felt like a product that's about to expire. After my first conflict with my mother, of course.

First night, I crashed into bed and fell asleep instantly ... my mom, and my best friend Lory woke me up, to make the bed ... so I woke up, I also changed into pyjamas, and a joke, I said to my mom, wont you tell me a bedtime story? what kind of a story she replied? any kind ... I'm just kiddin, mom ... I laid down in the bed and I was almost asleep, when I heard her sayin: I will tell you a story, about a little girl, who wants to know everything ... ... I had my confirmation right there, I was gettin NOTHING, but another bedtime story, again! Little girl!?! Wake up, mom, I`m fuckin' 34! I fell asleep instead ... I was somehow prepared for this ... I dreamed the whole shit, 2 or 3 weeks before we got there ... what was I to do? I know you're gonna fuck up again? So, I'm not takin' you with me? No. A good christian doesn't do that, mom! I never abandoned you, ever, even once, before you started abandoning me. And now you ask me, why can't I smile any more? Why am I not swallowing the shit any more? Simple. I had enough! Don't you agree? I dont need you any more!thanks for nothing! thanks for the lesson of not being able to trust anyone, not even the one that gave you life ... oh, no, that's God, the one that gave you birth ... or, whatever ... Is there at least one second when you didn't want to get rid of me?Why did you accept me in the first place? You thought he's gonna change his mind and leave his family for you? I was your secret weapon, your ace on the sleeve? Well, you lost! Big time! He fooled you, he used you. And now you're surprised I cut like a knife?!? You're surprised I win all the games I play?!? What am I to you??? What? A toy? a little girl? your friend? your mother? When am I your daughter? Ever? Never? To protect that stupid fuck, who is my biological father, you exposed your family. You made a shame of your family, to save his family. The only time you claimed me, is when anyone else threatened to take me away. You are now afraid to tell me the truth, but you weren't afraid to say it to Lory's mom. You trust her above

126

me, your own flesh and blood! How fucked up is this? Guess what, it's not me you don't trust ... it's you. Yes, the one you have to see in the mirror every day. When you looked at the pictures I took of you next to the Eiffel tower, you said you look as if you're dead. Well, that's because you are! I took you to the hairdresser, I gave you make-ups so you can make yourself look alive, at least on the outside. 3 years ago I payed your appointment with a psychologue, that was my teacher, you came with me, and you started cryin' outside his door, that your into too much pain! What about my pain, mom? Don't I have feelings? Don't I get hurt? I do. I get hurt, I bruise, I cry, I stumble, I fall but I pull myself together and I start walking again. That's life, mom. The one you gave me ... those were your projections on me. I am what you made of me. Thank you for everything. But now, you're afraid of me. Now you're afraid the game went too far. I remembered, I told you I won't bring up this subject again, that I'll just let you decide when you want to tell me the whole story. You started it, 4 years ago ... but not to me, to Lory's mom ... just like that, while you were having a coffee, in the kitchen. We had thousands of coffees ... everywhere ... just the two of us ... why haven't you found a way to tell me? am I too stupid to understand? am I unworthy of the truth?

Did you ever, for a second consider ... let me simplify this, did it ever occur to you, that by telling me the truth, you could spare me years of suffering, of going around in circles? or what? you enjoyed my suffering? you thought I deserve it?For what? For coming into this world? Was it a price I had to pay for daring to be your child? When will I deserve the truth? Your unconditional trust?

While in Paris, you haven't bought anything for your mom, your husband ... you bought gifts for your daughter in-law, for her kids .... you didn't give me anything, ..., you just left me some of the things I payed for, in the first place ... well ... the truth is ... I'm not for sale ... I'm a gift from God, a blessing, not a curse ... a reward, not a punishment. Sorry if you thought about this, this way, but that's your truth my our perception, your reality. Not mine. I don't lie. I don't fool myself in made-up stories. I don't kiss and make-up for everything. I'm not a child any more! Please accept and face that. I will always be your girl, but I'm an adult now. A grown up woman. A whole. Not just a part, when you think it's comfortable ... Aren't you proud of me? Where you were once weak, I am now strong. Isn't this what you prayed for? Well, God made your dreams come true. God answered your prayers! from ana-maria to maria-ana" (*end of the fragment in English in original without corrections*).

After she read the letter, Ana-maria also felt a moment of release; she was glad that, as she put it, "I did not cry", and she found a way "of saying goodbye" to the past. She said she had packed up all the diaries and stored them in a safe place; she did not need them any longer, she had selected what was necessary for her rebirth. She was adapted to the group she had joined, and the behaviours practised proved to be beneficial for her. The states of the Adult Ego supervised the other states of her ego, so she felt "down to earth". During one session with the new group, I asked her how she had appreciated the therapeutic relationship, if there was a moment when she felt revolted or strange (I was following her counter-transfer towards me). She said no, only once had she felt "abandoned", when she asked me if she could come with the new group. It was the moment when I let her decide to continue or not the group activity, then I as therapist felt her "game of abandoned child" and by the freedom of choice I made her liable from the position of Adult ego.

Final conclusions

The therapeutic objectives were reached from the perspective of the model proposed, but I could not have reached any of them unless I had built an authentic therapeutic relation. Ana-maria, who agreed to use this name, was motivated for her own therapy and allowed the exchange of materials: she gave me excerpts from her diaries, I offered her the possibility to complete my material. It was a permanent co-creation of the therapeutic relationship. I asked myself why I had chosen Ana-maria. I think it was my need to reach an objective related to my profession; somehow, by solving the "Ana-maria case", I feel as though I "picked up" some of the beauty of writing on psychotherapy. I was my own client from the professional viewpoint; I focused that external perspective on what I write, with analysis on writing, on what I can feel and on what the client does. Not all therapists write about their cases; they do not have the time and not all clients are willing to give such a feedback to the therapists.

The model offers an intervention pattern, the therapeutic relation is essential, the therapeutic objectives guided the therapist's activity. The Ana-maria case was a way of validating my model, a qualitative research to validate my model. The model offers the therapist freedom of intervention, the cultivation and accountability of the client in his or her own therapy, and if the client does not want to or cannot do it, the therapist focuses on the frame objectives. Each session may constitute an opportunity of intervention for approaching a category of objectives, but the foundation on which all objectives of the model are reached is the objective of the first category (creation of the therapeutic relationship). The model may be applied in individual therapy as well, or to a client belonging to a group. In the future I may attempt to approach the model with an entire group of participants.

The therapist is in the group what the participants want her to be, is there for all and for everyone. Any client may be the protagonist, as long as the group members agree, as long as the group supports the protagonist. The topics approached in the group are in fact ontological topics through which the self of each group participant is activated, the life path of the client, renarrated and relived, represents a modality of self-activation.

The group participants learned to analyse the relationing dynamics for each of them and supported the protagonist (not only client X.Z., but any client who was speaking). The clients were assisted in understanding the manner of being assertive, accepting their needs, observing the realities of the persons beside them. Love is a recurrent topic in the group and individual therapy. People often live with pain because they think they cannot be loved. Love means also a reunion of separation. The client is separated in his or her reality from the others or feels separated even from himself or herself. In the group they can find the outside world at a much more reduced scale; they find acceptance, unconditional closeness, without judgements and evaluations. There occurs a reunion of the client's separation from himself and the others, and a new attempt to re-enter the world.

The therapist and the group members work together to create a climate of mutual respect, mutual acceptance, necessary for building a relational empathy among the group members and in the interpersonal relations from outside the therapy group. Empathy and sympathy are managed by the therapist.

Each group led by the therapist is unique in its way, like the clients who ask for individual therapy, but they seem to remake, in their evolution during the ten sessions, the stages of human development: birth, growing up, maturity and dissolution of the group in the world outside the practice; the client comes from the external world and returns to it. The therapist may learn from each group both on the methodological plane and on the personal plane. The therapist enters the group therapy with all his or her knowledge and life experience, the main methodological instrument being the therapist *in se*. I believe that the strength of the therapist resides in the way he or she succeeds in being authentic and in inviting to self-development each member of the group and the group as a whole. The therapist is in the group at the same time for himself, for each group member and for the entire group. When the therapist succeeds in managing the roles simultaneously, he or she manages love, strength and group evaluation, and I consider that this is the moment when the group becomes mature.

The metaphoric techniques are useful after the group members get acquainted with one another, and, grace to the suggestions made, the therapist acts in the sense of enhancing the force of the Ego for the client, for the increase of self-esteem in the group participants. But what is essential is the therapcutic relationship co-created with the client and with the group as a whole, as an unseen relationship.

Bibliography

1.   Assagioli, R. A., (1976) *Psycho synthesis: A manual of principles and techniques.* N.Y.: HobbsDorman, 1965; Baltimore: Penguin
2.   Bandler, R., Grinder, J., (1975a), *Patterns of the Hypnotic Techniques of Milton H. Erickson*, M.D. Vol. 1. Meta Publications, Cupertino, California.
3.   Bandler, R., Grinder, J., (1975b), *The Structure of Magic: a book about language and therapy.* Palo Alto: Science and Behavioral Books.
4   Bandler, R., Grinder, I., (2007) *Tehnicile psihoterapiei ericksoniene,* Ed. Curtea Veche, Bucureşti
5.   Berne, E., (1961) *Transactional Analysis in Psychotherapy,* New York.
6.   Buber, M., (1967) *The Knowledge of Man.* New York: Harper and Row.
7.   Cădariu, L., (2003) *Management educaţional. Evaluarea comportamentului managerial al directorului de şcoală,* Ed. Mirton, Timişoara
8.   Clarkson, P., (1988), *Gestalt Therapy - An Up Date.* Self and Society, 16 (2), 74-79.
9.   Clarkson, P., (2003) *The therapeutic relationship (2nd ed.).* London: Whurr
10. Culley, S., Bond, T., (2004) *Integrative Counseling Skills in Action 2 nd.* Edition, London
11. Culley S., Bond, T., (2007), *Integrative Counselling Skills in Action, 2nd Edition,* SAGE Publications, London
12. Dafinoiu, I., . Vargha,J.L., (2003) *Hipnoza clinică. Tehnici inducţie. Strategii terapeutice,* Ed. Polirom, Iaşi
13. Dafinoiu, I., . Vargha,J.L., (2005) *Psihoterapii scurte,* Ed. Polirom, Iaşi
14. Dahlberg, K., Dahlberg, H., and Nystrom, M., (2008) *Reflective Lifeword Research (2 nd edition) Lund, Sweden:* Student literature

15. Dessache, H., (1986) *Autobiographie raisone et maientique de projets,* dans G. Pineau, G. Jobcrt, *Histoires de vie,* tome, Paris, Editrons L'harma Men

16. Shazer, S., (1985) *Keys to solution in Brief therapy* WW Norton & Company, Ney York;

17. Drobot, L., (2009) *Psihoterapie integrativă. Fundamente.,* Ed. V&I Integral, Bucureşti;

18. Drobot ,L., (2009) *Psihoterapie relaţională,* Ed. Mirton, Timişoara

19. Drobot, L., (2009) *Consiliere şi psihoterapie integrativă,* Ed. Mirton, Timişoara

20. Drobot, L., (2009), *Consiliere şi psihoterapie integrativă,* Editura Mirton, Timişoara.

21. Erickson, M.H., (1964) *The confusion technique in hypnosis.* American Journal of Clinical Hypnosis

22. Erickson, M.H., & Rossi, E., (1979) *Hypnotherapy: An Exploratory casebook.* New York: Irvington

23. Erskine, R. & Moursund, J., (1988) *Integrative psychotherapy in action.* Newbury Park, CA: Sage Publication 24. Evans, K., Gilbert, M., (2005) *An Introduction to Integrative Psychotherapy,* Palgrane Macmillan, New York

25. Evans, K., Finlay L., (2009) *Relational – centre Research for Psychotherapist. Exploring meanings and experience,* Sons, Ltd. Publication

26. Gerson, S., (2004) *The Relational Unconscious: A Care Element of Intersubjectivity, Tiredness and Clinical Process,* Psychoanalytic Quarterly, LXXIII

27. Maroda, K. (1991) *The Power of Transference.* New York: Jon Wilen&Yons. Inc.

28. Merleau – Ponty, M., (1968) *The Visible and the Invisible (Trans.A.Lingis) Evanston, IL:* Northwestern University Press Original Work Published in 1964

29. Todres, L., (2007) *Embodied Enquiry Phenomenological touchstones for research Psychotherapy and Spirituality,* Basingstoke, Hampshire: Palarave Macmillan

30. Yontef, G., (2002) *The relational attitude in gestalt theory and*

practice: International Gestalt. Journal, 25(1), pp.15-35

31. Yontef, G., M., (1988) *Assimilating Diagnostic and Psychoanalytical Perspectives into Gestalt Therapy.* Gestalt Journal, 11(1), p. 5-32

http://www.integrativetherapy.com/en/articles
http://www.integrativetherapy.com/fr/articles
http://www.sagepublications.com

Alexander, F., & French, T.M.,	(1946)	*Psychoanalytic therapy: Principles and applications,* New York: Ronald Press
Arkowitz,H.	(1992)	Integrative theories of therapy. In D.K. Freedheim(Ed.).History of psychotherapy: A century of change (p.261-303), Washington, D.C.: American Psychological Association
Arkowitz,H.,&Messer, S.B.	(1984)	Psychoanalytic therapy and behavior therapy: Is integration possible? New York: Plenum
Arlow, J.,	(1969)	Fantasy, memory, and reality testing. Psychoanalytic Quarterly,38, 28-51
Arlow, J.,	(1969)	Unconscious fantasy and disturbances of conscious experience. Psychoanalytic Quarterly, 38: 1-27.
Arnoff, D.B., & Glass, C.R,,	(1992)	Cognitive therapy and psychotherapy integration. In D.K. Freedheim(Ed.). History of psychotherapy (p.657-694). Washington, D.C.: American Psycho-logical Association.

Assagioli, R. A.,	(1976)	Psychosynthesis: A manual of principles and techniques. N.Y.: HobbsDorman, 1965; Baltimore: Penguin
Assagioli, R. A.,	(1974)	The act of will. N.Y.: Viking, 1973; Baltimore: Pengiun
Bach, S.,	(1985)	Narcissistic states and the therapeutic process. New York: Basic Books
Baker, E.	(1982)	The management of transference phenomena in the treatment of primitive states. Psychotherapy, Theory, Research and Practice, 19,194-197
Bary, B. & Hufford, F.,	(1990)	Understanding the six advantages to games and their use in treatment planning. Transactional Analysis Journal, 20 (40), 214-220
Basch, M.,	(1988)	Understanding psychotherapy: The science behind the art. New York: Basic Books
Basch, M.,	(1988)	Understanding psychotherapy: the science behind the art. New York: Basic Books
Benjamin, L.S.,	(1982)	Use of Structural Analysis of Social Behavior (SASB) to guide intervention in psychotherapy. In J.C. Anchin & D.J. Kiesler (Eds.), Handbook of interpersonal psychotherapy (pp. 190-212). New York: Pergamon
Berne, E.,	(1961)	Transactional Analysis in Psychotherapy, New York.

Berne, E.,	(1964)	Games people play: The psychology of human relationships. New York: Grove Press
Berne, E.,	(1966)	Principles of group treatment. New York: Grove Press
Bertalanffy, L. von	(1969)	General systems theory: Essays on its foundation and development (rev.ed.). New York: Braziller
Besser, L.,	(2000)	Psychotrauma. Workshop Presentation, Kassel
Beutler, L. E.,	(1983)	Eclectic psychotherapy: A systematic approach. Elmsford, NY: Pergamon Press
Bowlby, J.,	(1969)	Attachment. Volume I of Attachment and loss. New York: Basic Books
Bowlby, J.,	(1973)	Separation: anxiety and anger. Volume II of Attachment and loss. New York: Basic Books
Bowlby, J.,	(1973)	Attachment and loss. Vol.2, Separation, anxiety, and anger. New York: Basic Books.
Brenner, C.,	(1979)	Working alliance, therapeutic alliance, and transference. Journal of the American Psychoanalytic Association.
Bowlby, J.,	(1980)	Loss: sadness and depression. Volume III of Attachment and loss. New York: Basic Books
Bucke, R. M.,	(1923)	Cosmic consciousness, a study in the evolution of the human mind. New York: Dutton
Callahan, R.,	(1985)	Five Minute Phobia Cure, Indian

		Wells
Callahan, R.,	(1989)	The Anxiety – Addiction Connection: Eliminate Your Addictive Urges, Indian Wells
Cartwright, D.S. & Cartwright, R.D.	(1958)	Faith and improvement in psychotherapy. Journal of Counseling Psychology,5, 174-177
Clark, B.D.,	(1991)	Empathetic transactions in the deconfusing of Child ego states. Transactional Analysis Journal, 21, p.92-98
Clarkson, P.,	(2003)	The therapeutic relationship (2nd ed.). London: Whurr
Clarkson, P.,	(2005)	Psychotherapy as positive psychology. London: Whurr
Craig, G. & Fowlie, A.,	(1995 & 1997)	Emotional Freedom Techniques. The Manual
Cummings, N.A.,	(1995)	Impact of managed care on employment and trending: A primer for survival. Professional Psychology: Research and Practice, 26, 10-15.
Dimond, R.E., Havens, R.A., & Jones, A.C.	(1978)	A conceptual framework for the practice of prescriptive eclecticism in psychotherapy. American Psychologist, 33, 239-248.
Erikson, E.,	(1950)	Childhood and Society. New York: Norton

Erskine, R.,	(1980)	Script cure: behavioral, intrapsychic and physiological. Transactional Analysis Journal, 10, p. 102-106.
Erskine, R.,	(1988)	Ego structure, intrapsychic function, and defense mechanisms: A commentary on E. Berne's original theoretical concepts. Transactional Analysis Journal, 18, 15-19
Erskine, R.,	(1989)	A relationship therapy: Developmental perspectives. In B.R. Loria (Ed.), Developmental theories and the clinical process: Conference proceedings of the Eastern Regional Transactional Analysis conference (p.123-135). Madison, Wl: Omnipress
Erskine, R.,	(1991)	Transference and transactions: Critique from an intrapsychic and integrative perspective. Transactional Analysis Journal, 21(2), 63-76
Erskine, R.G.,	(1980)	Script cure: behavioral, intrapsychic and physiological. Transactional Analysis Journal.
Erskine, R.G.,	(1987)	A structural analysis of ego: Eric Berne's contribution to the theory of psychotherapy. In Keynote speeches: Delivered at the EATA conference, July, 1986, Noordwijkerhout, The Netherlands. Geneva, Switzerland: European Association for Transactional

Analysis

Erskine, R.G.,	(1997)	Trauma, dissociation and a reparative relationship. Australian Gestalt 76urnal, 1, p. 38-47
Erskine, R. & Moursund, J.,	(1988)	Integrative psychotherapy in action. Newbury Park, CA: Sage Publication
Erskine, R. & Trautmann, R.,	(1996)	Theories and Methods of an Integrative Transactional Analysis (TA Journal 26, 316-328), San Francisco
Erskine, R. & Zalcman, M.,	(1979)	The Racket System (TA Journal 9, 51-59), San Francisco
Fairbairn, W.R.D.,	(1952)	An Object-relations theory of the personality. New York: Basic Books
Federn, P.,	(1977)	Ego personality and the psychoses. London: Mareshfield Reprints. (Original work published 1953)
Fiedler, F.	(1950a)	The concept of an ideal therapeutic relationship. Journal of Consulting Psychology, 14,235-245
Fiedler, F.	(1950b)	A comparison of therapeutic relationship in psychoanalytic, nondirective and Adlerian therapeutic relationship. Journal of Consulting Psychology, 14,436-445
Fiedler, F.	(1951)	Factor analyses of psychoanalytic, nondirective and Adlerian therapeutic

		relationship. Journal of Consulting Psychology, 15, 32-38
Fish, J.M.	(1973)	Placebo therapy. San Francisco: Jossey-Bass.
Ford, D.H.,& Urban, H.B.,	(1963)	System of psychotherapy. New York: Wiley
Fraiberg, S.,	(1982)	Pathological defenses in infancy. Psychoanalytic Quarterly, 51, p. 612-635.
Frank, J.D.,	(1982)	Therapeutic components shared by all psychotherapies. In J.H. Harvey & M.M. Peeks (Eds.).Psychotherapy research and behavior change (p.9-37.)Washington, D.C.: American Psychological Association
Freud, A.,	(1936)	Ego and the Mechanisms of Defense, New York
Freud, S.,	(1905)	Three essays on the theory of sexuality, in The Standard Edition of the Complete psychological Works of Sigmund Freud. Vol. 7, London: Hogarth Press
Freud, S.,	(1961)	Beyond the pleasure principle. In J. Strachey (Ed. and Trans.), The standard edition of the complete psychological works of Sigmund Freud (Vol. 17). London: Hogarth Press. (Original work published 1923)

Freud, S.,	(1965)	Normality and pathology in childhood: Assessment of development. New York: International Universities Press
Garfield, S.L.,	(1980)	Psychotherapy: An eclectic approach, New York: John Wiley
Gelso, C.J. & Carter, J.A.,	(1985)	The relationship in counseling and psychotherapy: Components, consequences, and theoretical antecedents. The Counseling Psychologist, 13(2), 163.
Gelso, C.J., Mills, D.H., & Spiegel, S.B,	(1983)	Client and therapist factors influencing the outcome of time-limited counseling one and 18 months after treatment. In C.J. Gelso & D.H. Johnson, Explorations in time-limited counseling and psychotherapy (p. 296-306). New York: Teachers College Press
Gill, M.M.,	(1993)	Interaction and interpretation. Psychoanalytic Dialogues, 3, 111-122
Goldfried, M.R.,	(1980)	Toward the delineation of therapeutic change principles. American Psychologist, 35, 991-999

Goldfried, M.R., & Newman, C.,	(1986)	Psychotherapy integration: An historical perspective. In J.C. Norcross (Ed.), Handbook of eclectic psychotherapy (pp. 25-61). New York: Brunner/ Mazel
Goldstein, K.	(1939)	The organism. New York: Harcourt Brace Jovanovich
Greenberg, J.R. et. Mitchell, S.A.,	(1983)	Object relation in psychoanalytic theory. Cambridge, MA: Harvard University Press
Greenson, R.R.	(1967)	The technique and practice of psychoanalysis. New York: International University Press
Grof, S.,	(1979)	Realms of the human unconsciousness. London: Souvenir Press
Guntrip, H.,	(1971)	Psychoanalytic Theory, Therapy and the Self. New York: Basic Books
Held, B.S.,	(1984)	Toward a strategic eclecticism: a proposal: Psychotherapy, 21, 232-241
Horowitz, M.,	(1987)	States of mind: Analysis of change in psychotherapy (2nd ed.). New York: Plenum
Hycner, R.,	(1993)	Between person and person: Toward a dialogical relationship. London: Gestalt Journal Press.

Jahoda, M.,	(1958)	Current concepts of mental health. New York: Basic Books
Johnson, M.E., Popp, C., Schacht, T.E., Mellon, J., & Strupp, H.H.	(1989)	Converging evidence for identification of recurrent relationship themes: Comparison of two methods. Psychiatry, 52, 275-288
Jung, C.G.,	(1928)	Analytical psychology and education. In Contributions to analytical psychology (H.G. & C.F. Baynes, Trans.). London:Kegan Paul, Trench, Trubner.
Jung, C.G.,	(1966)	The psychology of the transference. In Collected works (Vol. 16, pp. 162-323). London: Routledge & Kegan Paul. (Original work published 1946)
Kahn, M.M.R.	(1963)	The concept of cumulative trauma. Psychoanalytic Study of the Child, 18, p. 286-301
Kohlenberg, R.J., & Tsai, M.,	(1991)	FAP: Functional analytic psychotherapy. New York: Plenum
Kohut, H.,	(1971)	The Analysis of the Self. New York: International Universities Press
Kohut, H.,	(1977)	The Restoration of the Self. New York: International Universities Press
Lambert, M.J., & Bergin, A.E.	(1994)	The effectiveness of psychotherapy. In A.E. Bergin & S.L. Garfield (Eds). Handbook of psychotherapy and behavior

		change (4th Ed., p. 143-189).New York: Wiley.
Lammers,W.,	(1999)	Successive Point Protocol. Workshop Presentation, Maienfeld
Langs, R.,	(1976)	The therapeutic intervention: Vol. II. A critical overview and synthesis. New York: Jason Aronson
Langs, R.,	(1981)	Classics in psychoanalytic techniques. New York: Plenum
Lazarus, A.A.,	(1976)	In support of technical eclecticism. Psychological Reports, 21, 415-416.
Lazarus, A.A., Beutler, L.E., & Norcross, J.C.,	(1992)	The future of technical eclecticism. Psychotherapy, 29, 11-20
Levenson, H., & Strupp, H.H.,	(1999)	Recommendations for the future of trending in brief dynamic psychotherapy. Journal of Clinical Psychology, 55, 385-391
Lipton, S.,	(1977)	The advantages of Freud's technique as shown in his analysis of the rat man. International Journal of Psychoanalysis, 58, 255-273.
Loria, B.R.,	(1988)	The parent ego state: Theoretical foundations and alterations. Transactional Analysis Journal, 18:1
Lourie, J.,	(1996)	Cumulative trauma: the nonproblem problem. Transactional Analysis Journal,

		26, p. 276-283
Luborsky, L.,	(1984)	Principles of psychoanalytic psychotherapy: A manual for supportive-expressive treatment. New York: Basic Books
Lyons-Ruth, K., & Jacobwitz, D.,	(1999)	Attachment disorganization: Unresolved loss, relational violence, and lapses in behavioral and attention strategies. In J. Cassidy & P.R. Shaver, Handbook of attachment: Theory, research, and clinical applications (p. 520-554). New York: Guilford
Mahler, M.,	(1967)	The goals of psychotherapy. Englewood Cliffs, NJ: Prentice-Hall. Marmor , J. (1976). Common operational factors in diverse approaches to behavior change. In A. Burton (Ed.).What makes behavior change possible? (p.160-194). New York: Brunner/ Mazel.
Mahler, M.,	(1968)	On human symbiosis and the vicissitudes of individuation. New York: International Universities Press
Mahler, M., Pine, F., & Bergman, A.,	(1975)	The psychological birth of the human infant. Symbiosis and individuation. New York: Basic Books

Maslow, A.H	(1956)	Self-actualizing people: A study of psychological health. In C.E. Moustakis (Ed.). The Self: Explorations in personal growth, (p.3-12). New York: Harper& Row
Maslow, A.H.,	(1970)	Motivation and personality (2nd ed.). New York: Viking Press
Maslow, A.H.,	(1970)	Religions, values, and peakexperiences. New York: Viking Press
Maslow, A.H.,	(1972)	The farther reaches of human nature. New York: Viking
McNeel, J.R.,	(1976)	The parent interview. Transactional Analysis Journal, 6:1
Mearns, D., & Thorne, B.,	(2002)	Person-centred counseling in action. London: Sage
Messer, S.B.,	(1992)	A critical examination of belief structures in integrative and eclectic psychotherapy. In J.C. Norcross& M.R. Goldfried (Eds.), Handbook of psychotherapy integration (p. 130-159). New York: Basic Books
Messer, S.B.,	In press	Applying the visions of reality to a case of brief therapy. Journal of Psychotherapy Integration

Norcross, J.C., (1986) Handbook of eclectic psychotherapy. New York: Brunner/Mazel

Orlinsky, D.E.,& Howard, K.I., (1986) Process and outcome in psychotherapy. In S.L. Garfield & A.E. Bergin (Eds.). Handbook of psychotherapy and behavior change (3rd ed., p. 311-384). New York: Wiley

Ornstein, A., (1989, October) Countertransference in a intersubjective perspective: A case presentation. Panel discussion, 12th annual conference on the psychology of the self, San Francisco

Ouspensky, P.D., (1949) In search of the miraculous. New York: Harcourt Brace

Parloff, M.B., (1967) Goals in psychotherapy: Mediating and ultimate. In A.R. Mahrer (Ed.). The goals of psychotherapy (p.5-19). Englewood Cliffs, N.J.: Prentice-Hall

Patterson, C.H., (1985a) The therapeutic relationship: Foundations for an eclectic psychotherapy. Pacific Grove, CA: Brooks /Cole

Patterson, C.H., (1985b) What is the placebo in psychotherapy? Psychotherapy, 22,163-169.

Patterson, C.H.,	(1989)	Eclecticism in psychotherapy: Is integration possible? Psychotherapy, 26,157-161
Pedersen, P.	(1976)	The field of intercultural counseling. In P. Pedersen, W.J .Lonner, & J.G. Draguns (Eds). Counseling across cultures. Honolulu: University Press of Hawaii
Pentony, P.,	(1981)	Models of influence in psychotherapy. New York: Free Press
Perls, F.S.,	(1944)	Ego, hunger and aggression: A revision of Freud's theory and method. Durban, RSA: Knox Publishing
Perls, F.S., & Baumgardner, P.,	(1975)	Legacy from Fritz: Gifts from Lake Cowichan. Palo Alto, CA: Science & Behavior Books
Perls, F.S., Hefferline, R., & Goodman, P.,	(1951)	Gestalt therapy: Excitement and growth in the human personality. New York: Julian Press
Piaget, J.,	(1932)	The moral judgment of the child. New York: Harcourt Press
Piaget, J.,	(1951)	Play, dreams and imitation in childhood. New York: Norton
Piaget, J.,	(1954)	The construction of reality in the child. New York: Basic Books
Polster, E., & Polster, M.,	(1973)	Gestalt therapy integrated: Contours of theory and practice. New York: Random House

Quintana, S.M., & Meara, N.M.,	(1990)	Internalization of the therapeutic relationship in short term psychotherapy. Journal of Counseling Psychology, 37, 123-130
Reich, W.,	(1945)	Character analysis. New York: Farrar, Strauss & Giroux
Robertson, M.,	(1979)	Some observations from an eclectic therapist. Psychotherapy: Theory, Research, and Practice, 16, 18-21
Rogers, C.R.,	(1951)	Client-centered therapy: Its current practice, implications and theory Boston: Houghton Mifflin
Rogers, C.R.,	(1956)	Client-centered therapy: A current view. In F. Fromm – Reichmann & J.L. Moreno (Eds.). Progress in psychotherapy:1956 New York: Grune & Stratton
Rogers, C.R.,	(1957)	The necessary and sufficient conditions of therapeutic personality change. Journal of Consulting Psychology, 21, 95-103
Rogers, C.R.,	(1959)	A theory of therapy, personality and interpersonal relationships, as developed in the client-centered framework. In S. Koch (Ed.) Psychology: A study of a science. Vol. 3: Formulations of the person and social context (p184-256). New York:

MacGraw-HILL

Rogers, C.R.,	(1961)	On becoming a person. Boston: Houghton Mifflin
Rosenthal, D., & Frank, J.D.,	(1956)	Psychotherapy and the placebo effect. Psychological Bulletin, 53, 294-302
Rosenzweig, S.,	(1936)	Some implicit common factors in diverse methods of psychotherapy. American Journal of Orthopsychiatry, 6, 412-415
Rowan, J.,	(2004)	Three levels of therapy. Counseling and Psychotherapy Journal, 15(9), 21
Riemann, F.,	(1984)	Grundformen der Angst. Eine tiefenpsychologische Studie. München/ Basel
Safran, J.D., & Segal, Z.V.,	(1990)	Interpersonal process in cognitive therapy. New York: Basic Books
Samuels, A., Shorter, B., & Plaut, F.,	(1986)	A critical dictionary of Youngian analysis. London: Routledge & Kegan Paul
Sandler, J.,	(1976)	Countertransference and role-responsiveness. International Review of Psycho-Analysis, 3, 43-47
Shapiro, F.,	(1995)	Eye Movement Desensitization and Reprocessing. Basic Principles, Protocols and Procedures, New York

Skinner, B.F.,	(1958)	Reinforcement today. American Psychologist, 14, 94-99
Smith, M.B.,	(1973)	Comment on White's paper. The Counseling Psychologist, 42, 48-50
Snygg, D.,& Combs, A.W.,	(1949)	Individual behavior: Anew frame of reference for psychology. New York: Harper
Spotnitz, H.,	(1969)	Modern psychoanalysis of the schizophrenic patient. New York: Grune et. Stratton
Stern, D.,	(1985)	The Interpersonal World of the Infant. New York: Basic Books
Stern, D.,	(1985)	The interpersonal world of the infant: a view from psychoanalysis and developmental psychology. New York: Basic Books
Storolow, R.D., Brandschaft, B., & Atwood, G.E,	(1987)	Psychoanalytic treatment: an intersubjective approach. Hillsdale, NJ: The Analytic Press
Strupp, H.H.,	(1980a)	Success and failure in time-limited psychotherapy: A systematic comparison of two cases (Comparison 1). Archives of General Psychiatry, 37, 595-603
Strupp, H.H.,	(1980b)	Success and failure in time-limited psychotherapy: A systematic comparison of two cases (Comparison 2). Archives of General Psychiatry, 37, 708-

716

Strop, H.H., & Binder, J.L.,	(1984)	Psychotherapy in a new key. New York: Basic Books
Sullivan, H.S.,	(1953)	The interpersonal theory of psychiatry. New York: W.W. Norton
Trautmann, R.,	(1985)	Letter from editor. Transactional Analysis Journal, 15, 188-191.
Trautmann, R., & Erskine, R.G.,	(1981)	Ego state analysis: A comparative view. Transactional Analysis Journal, 11, 178-185
Trower, P., Casey, A., & Dryden, W.,	(2003)	Cognitive behavioral counseling in action. London: Sage
Truax, C.B.,& Carkhuff, R.R.,	(1967)	Toward effective counseling and psychotherapy. Chicago: Aldine
Vargiu, J.,	(1974)	"Subpersonalities". Synthesis, Vol. 1
Vargiu, J.,	(1975)	"The observer and the consciousness of"I"". Synthesis, Vol. 1, p.94-100
Wachtel, P.L.,	(1997)	Psychoanalysis, behavior therapy, and the relational world. Washington, D.C.: American Psychological Association
Weil, Th.,	(1985)	Haw to Deal with Resistance in Psychotherapy (TA Journal 15, 159-163), San Francisco
Weiss., & Sampson, H.,	(1986)	The psychoanalytic process: Theory, clinical observation and empirical research. New York: Guilford
Winnicott, D.W.,	(1965)	The maturational process and the facilitating environment:

		studies in the theory of emotional development. New York: International Universities Press
Wolf, E.S.,	(1988)	Treating the self: elements of clinical self psychology. New York: Guilford Press
Wolfe, T.,	(1976)	The "ME" decade. New York Magazine. August 23, p.26-60
Wolpe, J.,	(1973)	The practice of behavior therapy (2nd ed.). New York: Paragon Press

Milton Keynes UK
Ingram Content Group UK Ltd.
UKHW021311011223
433627UK00026B/1030